Living Without a Safety Net

Tim Grant

Onwards and Upwards Publishers

3 Radfords Turf
Cranbrook
Exeter
EX5 7DX

www.onwardsandupwards.org

ISBN: 978-1-911086-35-2
Typeface: Sabon LT
Graphic design: LM Graphic Design

Unless otherwise indicated, Scripture quotations are taken from THE HOLY BIBLE, NEW INTERNATIONAL VERSION®, NIV® Copyright © 1973, 1978, 1984, 2010 by Biblica, Inc.™ Used by permission. All rights reserved worldwide.

Scripture quotations marked (NASB) are taken from the NEW AMERICAN STANDARD BIBLE Copyright © 1960, 1963, 1963, 1968, 1971, 1972, 1973, 1975, 1979, 1995 by Lockman Foundation.

Scripture quotations marked (MSG) are taken from THE MESSAGE. Copyright © by Eugene H. Peterson 1993, 1994, 1995, 1996, 2000, 2001, 2002. Used by permission of NavPress. All rights reserved. Represented by Tyndale House Publishers, Inc.

Disclaimer: The events in this book are written from the perspective of the author and how he remembers them. He has sought to present a factual account.

Endorsements

This book tells the story of what can happen to us all if we will simply follow the leadings of the Holy Spirit. Tim has done this.

Follow him through the triumphs and valleys that he has traversed to know Him who is invisible. A must read to stir up your faith in these end times.

Ian Andrews

This is a great account of Tim's life and ministry. It inspires all of us to remain loyal and faithful to the calling of God. This Tim has done (and continues to do) over all these years. Knowing Tim as I do I am sure there will be much more to be written in the coming years.

Derek Brown

Acknowledgements

My thanks go to all those people who have been part of our lives over the years without whose support, teaching and encouragement we would not be where we are today. They are just too many to mention by name here.

To Kim, my wife,
who has supported me through all the
ups and downs of our journey together.

Without her support I would not have
travelled so far in God and this book
would not have come into being.

Living Without a Safety Net

Contents

Living Without a Safety Net

FOREWORD BY PAUL MANWARING

I remember the first time that I heard of Tim Grant. It was at a regional gathering of leaders and, as is common, my wife had been chatting to various people. At one point she came excitedly to tell me of this man that she had met. He had been saying how blessed he was to be connected to us and to Bethel Church and how wonderful and encouraging the testimonies which he had heard coming from us were. Modestly he was saying that his stories didn't match up but as he told my wife some of his stories she assured him that his were some of the most amazing she had ever heard. I am delighted that they are now in a book and we can all be blessed and encouraged by this humble yet powerful man.

Reading through this manuscript I was delighted to see the inclusion of the story of the sheets. It is my favourite testimony of being obedient to the still, small voice of God and the rewards of a life of obedience. I will not spoil it by retelling it in this foreword but suffice it to say that it is the very essence of this man and this book. He was not the only one to hear God say the same thing but he was the one who obeyed.

This obedience is evident as a lifestyle as I read the story of Tim spitting on his thumbs and rubbing the eyes of a lady with tunnel vision. O my, who does that! Tim gives us the answer: men with no safety net who hear and obey.

Who, too, still buys tents that seat thousands and drives them across Europe to preach the Gospel of the Kingdom? Obedient men who have a history of hearing, risking, trusting and obeying, whether it be small or large, easy or difficult. Tim teaches us again.

I know perhaps of a few who could write a book entitled 'Living Without a Safety Net' but I have a very strong belief that there will be many more living that way as a result of reading this book.

I am humbled as I read it, challenged to an upgrade in my desire to trust and obey. Yes, the simple words of that old hymn have stood the test of time and are given a new lease of life in this beautifully written book.

When we walk with the Lord
In the light of His Word,
What a glory He sheds on our way;
While we do His good will,
He abides with us still,
And with all who will trust and obey.

Trust and obey,
For there's no other way
To be happy in Jesus,
But to trust and obey.

It is a book which leaves me with the title of Francis A. Schaeffer's book ringing in my ears: 'How should we then live?' Tim has showed us the way, the challenge is clear, listen and obey.

This book is not one of ideas, it is a life lived with one thing in mind and that is to do what Jesus told us and the Holy Spirit continues to tell us. We need no other safety net than Jesus.

Paul Manwaring
Member of the Senior Team
Bethel Church
Redding, California, USA

Author of 'What On Earth is Glory'
　　　　'Kisses from a Good God' (Destiny Image Publishing)

PROLOGUE

AS A YOUNG MAN I EXPERIENCED an open vision one Sunday morning in church. I say 'open vision' because it was so real that I was not entirely sure if I was still physically sat in the church building or had indeed been transported elsewhere!

I saw myself falling into a pit. As I tumbled through space I could see that the walls of the pit were steep and that the chasm was deep; it took some time for me to fall to the bottom. On reaching the floor I became aware that I was surrounded by prison doors, all of which were open. I had the overwhelming sense that I was there to somehow help those who had been imprisoned in this place to find a way to the surface where I could see the light of the sun was shining.

In the blink of an eye I was back at the surface and was aware that I was standing on a battlefield with smoke-filled air. There was a sense that a great victory had been won there. Soldiers were walking purposefully across the field and they were silhouetted against the sun.

As I watched them I was suddenly transported from the field and became aware that I was standing in the throne room of heaven. The sun that was shining on me was the light of my Lord and a voice boomed around me, "You have been commissioned." With these words still ringing in my ears the open vision ceased and I was once again seated in church. From that day I knew that I had been called to preach the Gospel.

CHAPTER ONE

Humble Beginnings

I WAS BORN IN FARNBOROUGH in the late fifties on a council estate that in later years was known for its high crime rate, and several of the children I played with in my younger days ended up spending time detained in prison at Her Majesty's pleasure.

My father was the youngest of a large local family and he and his brother Robert were well known around the town for their various escapades which usually ended in them getting a thrashing from the local 'bobby'. How times have changed! One of their favourite tricks was to row the local reservoir keeper's boat out into the middle of the water and scuttle it while swimming back to the shore to recover their clothes which they would leave in a neat pile on the bank. Of course you can only get away with this so many times before the keeper becomes wise and plots his revenge! Which is exactly what he did when one summer's day they returned to the bank to find that their clothes were missing and the keeper chased them dripping in their birthday suits across the common to their home where they were thoroughly punished for their misdemeanours.

Mum was brought up in Wokingham, again part of a large family. She became a nurse at Courtbourne Maternity Home in Albert Road in Farnborough, which is where she met my father and they married in April of 1946.

I was the youngest of four children, my eldest brother David having died early in his first year of life as a result of having been born suffering from spina bifida. We siblings only learnt of David's existence many years later. In hindsight you could see this tragedy had greatly affected my parents and explained why my father would become sad at certain times of the year. They were good people who loved us and worked hard to provide for us whilst caring for their ageing relatives.

In my fourth year we moved to my grandfather's small holding in Wokingham to care for him as my grandmother had died and he wasn't coping very well with looking after himself. We lived there for several years and it was a great place to grow up. I remember well sitting with my brother Derek and sister Jane in the feed shed trying to kill the rats which frequented the wooden building by pushing the sacks of chicken feed from the stack, hoping to crush the vermin below. Many a happy hour spent!

I continued the family tradition of getting wet when my cousin Pip stood me by the pond in Grandad's garden to take my picture with a Box Browning camera which had no adjustment on the focal length. Having naively responded to the order to "go back", I stepped back into the water, much to the delight of those around. I was nothing if not gullible!

This fun period in our lives came to an end when, due to a deteriorating relationship between my parents and Grandad, we were forced to move out within two days.

Fortunately, since 1947 Dad was employed as an electrician at the Royal Aircraft Establishment in Farnborough and was able to arrange a tied house for us to move into. Everything we possessed, which wasn't very much, was moved on the local coalman's small flatbed lorry to our new home in Marrowbrook Lane. This was quite a disruptive period in our lives, which included losing friends, with no opportunity to even say goodbye.

The house was quite small and the bath sited at the far end of the kitchen with a board placed on top to make a seat so we children could sit at the kitchen table for our meals. It was some years later that the government decided to knock the coal store and toilet into one and create a bathroom – such luxury!

My father had suffered hearing loss during the Second World War and progressively lost the ability to hear altogether during my childhood. He had been a tail gunner in Wellington bombers until medically retired in 1942. Returning from a sortie with the aircraft limping home having been shot up, the tail section broke off on landing and spilled Dad across the airfield. This and the noise of the flak in his turret had brought about his hearing impediment.

This caused more than a few problems and misunderstandings between us as I grew up. I had wire braces on my teeth for several years, courtesy of the orthodontist, which distorted the way my mouth formed words. This resulted in Dad often being unable to lip-read what I was saying and so he would rely on reading my facial expressions and body language which often led to him getting the wrong end of the stick. Both of us became increasingly frustrated with this situation and with each other, and it often erupted into arguments.

School was a difficult place for me as the new kid suddenly parachuted in when everyone had already formed their friendship circles. I was not very academically minded and showed little interest in sports so it was hard to find common ground with my new peers or indeed my teachers. Even when I tried, I didn't seem to be able to win! On one occasion I was sent to the headmaster's office to show him a banjo I had made during Arts and Crafts which had impressed my teacher. It's amazing what you can construct out of an old biscuit tin, a length of wood and some fishing line; Blue Peter, eat your heart out! I sat outside the school office, not an unusual occurrence as I visited often having been caught in various transgressions, and waited to be called in to show him my achievement. He arrived back to his office, called me in, and without even enquiring after the purpose of my current visit administered six of the best with the cane on my hands. I returned to the classroom somewhat upset at the injustices of life, wondering at the point of achieving anything at school as it appeared to my young self that I couldn't do anything right. Returning home that evening with a letter of apology from the school, I felt that at least my parents would stand up for me and would make a fuss. Imagine my disappointment when they let the school off the hook by declaring that I probably deserved the cane for some offense the school hadn't caught me committing! Rough justice indeed!

I became a target for bullying throughout my school life and I often returned home bruised and beaten. Anti-bullying policies were still many years off.

Shortly after I arrived at secondary school my parents were called in to be told that their youngest son was not very bright and all the school could hope to achieve during my time with them was to teach me some very basic reading skills and hopefully enough Maths to be able to count my wages. They encouraged my parents not to expect too much and that they should be able to get me a job filling up the shelves in Finefare, the local supermarket, when I eventually left school. This did little to endear the teachers to me and my bolshie attitude didn't help. I was in my History class one afternoon, when the teacher threw the board rubber at the boy next to me who wasn't paying attention. His aim was poor and the missile hit me instead. I picked it up and at his instruction, "Give it back to me, Grant," I did just that and let fly. Sadly, my aim was better than his and the wooden missile found its target. And once again I found myself waiting outside a headmaster's office!

All this did little to improve my attitude at school or give me any sense of self-worth. Leaving school in my sixteenth year was a relief, although I had achieved more than anyone had expected. There were bright spots during those five years, however. In an effort to escape the bullying at break times I would visit the library and help the librarian Mrs. Foster tidy the books. She was a kind lady who always encouraged me to do more. The school also recruited a special needs teacher who similarly encouraged me and enabled me to improve my rudimentary reading and writing skills.

Sadly, despite their hopes, they had not managed to teach me to spell. My first job working as a typesetter in a printing firm came to an abrupt end two months in when a job came in with bad spelling throughout. I copied it word for word including all the spelling mistakes, unable as I was to either spot or correct the errors.

Looking back, I believe that God was at work in my life even then to bring about His plans for me. Having lost this job, my father insisted I took the entrance exam for an apprenticeship with the Gas Board which I failed and was called out with all the others who had fallen short to be sent home. As I was leaving, the man in charge beckoned me over because he recognized my name; my brother Derek was already with the Gas Board and doing well. He was reading through my completed exam script. "Surely," he exclaimed, "you know the answer to this question?" and promptly instructed me to correct my paper. He repeated the process for three or four more questions after which he told me to return to the room with the successful candidates as I had now passed the entrance exam. Such kindness seemed very odd to me at the time but I was pleased once again to be in employment and receiving some training.

It was at this time that I met a man on the street who had bullied me throughout my time at secondary school and again was intent on threatening me. The thought came to mind, "If I let this carry on now, it will happen for the rest of my life." In that moment I decided things were going to change and instead of running away, I stood up to him and gave him the beating he had expected to give me. Things *were* changing! My newfound confidence meant that one day when the frustrations between my father and I overflowed into an argument, I squared up to him; and my mother, always seeking to keep the peace, had to step in between us to stop me thumping him. This led, as you might expect, to me being invited to move out of the home.

CHAPTER TWO

Fresh Start

OUR FAMILY HAD ONLY EVER attended church for christenings, weddings, funerals and scout parades so it wasn't until I was at secondary school that I came into any meaningful contact with Christians. At this point, having attended a Baptist church several times, I quickly dismissed them as nice people but a little weird. It wasn't until some years later when I was in my late teens that I again came across another group of Christians.

Like many young men of that era – short on cash and wanting to make a big impression – my preferred mode of transport was a motorbike. Within the group I hung out with, the main topics of conversation were bikes and girls. There was nothing we enjoyed more than riding around in large groups with the latest girl of our dreams on the back of our bikes; most of us aspired to imitate the bikers Dennis Hopper and Peter Fonda had played in such films as 'Easy Rider'.

So God really did not show up on my radar. Not until one particular 'girl of my dreams' seemed to spend far too much of her time going to church. This often left a group of us sitting on our bikes outside the local parish church waiting for her to appear after the evening service before we could head off to the local disco or pub for the night. It was while we were sitting there one particular Sunday evening that we started to discuss church and what it might be that kept drawing her back to this archaic building. After some discussion

17

it was suggested that she must have another boyfriend who went to the church and so was two-timing me. Even though I dismissed the suggestion as 'rubbish' with much bravado, the seed of doubt had been sown and began troubling my youthful mind.

The following week I decided that I would go to the church service to check out any competition, whether imaginary or not, and put them straight on a few things. To my relief there was clearly no one else I needed to worry about as the church was full of mainly older middle class people. As far as I was concerned that was the last time I needed to endure one of their terminally boring services. Later that evening as I dropped my girlfriend back at her house, her mother invited me in, sat me down and told me that she had been asked not to bring me to church again as some of the older people did not think I was the "right sort of person" for their church.

I wondered if my long hair, leather motorcycle jacket, scruffy jeans and the fact that I roared up to the church on my motorbike had anything to do with that! Of course, whether this was a genuine request from the old folk or just a clever ruse to get me back into church I may never know! However, I am sure that it had the effect that God intended as the next week I was back in church. If they didn't want me there I was going to go just to wind them up. I even started to go to events that they ran for the youngsters of the church as at this group I felt I was a bit of a celebrity; the biker amongst all these middle class kids.

The youth workers Alan and Ruth were an accepting and loving young Welsh couple whom I had decided were 'OK' even though they were more overt in their Christian beliefs than any of the other Christians I had met amongst this group. They told me that God loved me and wanted to be my friend. This was all a little strange for me but it was part of my girlfriend's life and I enjoyed winding the Christians up, so I continued to attend.

Some months later they invited me to see a Christian film called 'The Cross and the Switchblade' which was being shown at the local technological college. The film was about a gang in America and as it sounded fun, I agreed to go along. As I watched the tale unfold before me, I was impacted by the thought that the star of the film was living my life and although he was a few years ahead of me on his journey, the things that this gang were into were happening around me and I knew that I was heading down the same path. When towards the end of the film he declared that he knew there was a God who loved and cared for him, I was shocked. As I was riding away on my bike that evening, the truth dawned. "Oh God, there must be a God!" I knew immediately that if God existed then He must have a plan for my life and I realised that I did not have a clue what that involved.

Thinking back to my previous limited experience of Christianity at school I remembered that baptism was considered important so I went along to see the parish vicar Ben Hutchinson who encouraged me to be confirmed. But deep inside I knew I needed to be baptised and told him this. I had just read Acts 2:38: "Peter said to them, 'Repent and let each of you be baptised in the name of Jesus Christ for the forgiveness of your sins and you shall receive the gift of the Holy Spirit.'" I explained to Ben that there seemed to be an order here and as I had gotten things wrong up until now, I wanted to make sure that I now got it right. Ben encouraged me to go and see the local Baptist minister, Mike Pusey. I thank God for Ben who probably realised that he would never see me at his church again but recognised what I needed.

Mike, the pastor at Queens Road Baptist Church at that time, took one look at me and also seemed reluctant to baptise me immediately but suggested I talked with their youth leader, Bill Rice.

At this point I started to go along to services at the Baptist church, where I felt accepted by the warm and friendly people who expressed their love for God through lively worship with dancing and playing all sorts of instruments. It was loud and fun and seemed to me to be much more relevant than anything I had experienced to that point. I also spotted my old school librarian, Mrs. Foster, in the congregation, which made me feel at home.

Sometime later I was baptised and came up from the water to the congregation singing what had become my favourite chorus: "We are one in the Spirit." As I stood there they started to pray for me to receive the second baptism. I didn't have a clue what they were talking about and wondered if they thought I needed dunking again because of my background. After a short prayer I was encouraged to leave the pool so I guessed that they had decided I was 'OK' after all! I climbed up the steps from the baptismal pool and hugged my girlfriend who was holding my towel. As we embraced I felt as if I was lifted into the clouds. For weeks I was walking on air. I knew God loved me and I was in love with Him and the girl of my dreams. Our relationship was growing deeper and we had decided to get married at some point in the future. Everything was wonderful. Of course the combination of my newfound loves meant I spent less and less time with my biker friends which, on reflection, was sad because they needed the relationship I had found with God as well. Yet their reluctance to even look into my new faith seemed to drive a wedge between us and cause an even greater gap to grow in our friendships.

Things eventually settled down into a routine. On Sundays I would drop my girlfriend at the parish church and then shoot down on my bike to the service at the Baptist church as she did not feel comfortable with their more exuberant style of worship. We would always meet up after the services at the parish youth group.

It was because of this routine that I arrived late at the service at the Baptist church one Sunday evening and ended up sitting right at the back with no one on either side of me. As the minister was preaching I heard a voice talking to me, which shocked me as I had thought I was on my own there. I sat up and looked to see who it was but there was no one there! I decided that I must have been daydreaming and determined to pay more attention to the speaker. No sooner had I done this than the voice started to speak to me again. It was my own Eli and Samuel experience.[1]

The voice said, "You need to make a decision here and now. Which is more important to you: your love for Me or your love for your girlfriend?" I knew in a moment that God had been taking second place in my life ever since I became a Christian. It was something I had felt Him talking to me about many times previously but had been unwilling to take any action on the subject. Now He was facing me up. He told me that I would never do the things He had planned for me to do if my love for Him was half-hearted. Father God was challenging me and as Jesus explained to Peter in the scripture, "...everyone who has left houses or brothers or sisters or father or mother or children or farms for My name's sake, will receive many times as much, and will inherit eternal life."[2]

---

[1] See 1 Samuel 3
[2] Matthew 19:29 (NASB)

I knew that night that I had to end my relationship with my girlfriend but almost everything in me wanted to continue it. As soon as we met later that evening, she asked me what was wrong as she could see I was upset. As I shared what had happened earlier in the evening, we hugged and cried as both of us knew we had to end our relationship but neither wanted to. When I left her that night I fell from the clouds into a pit of despair. I could not believe what I had done and over the coming weeks tried to get back together with her, but after what she had seen in my face that night she did not even want to talk with me.

Weeks and months went by while I was angry with God because of the choice He had given me to make. I went back to my old friends but could no longer find happiness with them. This culminated with going away for a weekend's biking around the West Country. We were in a pub for the evening and I had to leave, I felt so desperate. I sat outside on a bench on the village green contemplating suicide, asking myself why it was that God had left me.

I heard the voice again, this time in my head. He said, "Turn around."

I retorted, "That's what's brought me to this place, turning around and following You!"

The voice repeated His instruction, "Turn around and look behind you."

As I did I noticed a banner high on a wall which declared, "If God seems far away, guess who moved?" In that moment of time I knew that He had brought me to this place even while I was trying to run away from Him. That night I determined that I had already given God the one thing I valued more than anything else in life and it was foolish to now distance myself from Him. He surely couldn't expect anything greater from me. I knew that I needed to trust that God's plan would lead me into the abundant life Jesus declared that He had come into this world to enable each of us to have.[3]

Looking back, I realise that this was the first step of faith that I had ever taken; making that choice to trust Him with the rest of my life. Up until this point my faith had been about obedience to God's commands. After all, He is GOD and I am just one of His created

---

[3] See John 10:10

beings! But from that night it became more about trusting Him and giving over the direction of my life to Him. It was from this point that I started the journey that continues even to this day, which is to become everything that God intended me to be and to have that rich, fulfilling and overflowing life that He has always planned for each of us to have.

CHAPTER THREE

Hope for the Future

DURING THESE EARLY MONTHS of my faith, Alan and Ruth suggested to me that I might benefit from attending a major youth event called Eurofest '75 which was about to take place in Brussels, Belgium. Little could they have known the impression this conference would make on my life!

So together with Pete, another newly saved guy, we set off on my Suzuki 250GT motorbike to join some fifteen thousand other young people from around the world to listen and learn from the great men and women who had come to teach and inspire us from their experience. We very nearly didn't make it as we ran out of petrol before we even got to the port and ended up pushing the bike several miles until we found a petrol station. We missed our ferry at Dover and had to race over the hills to Folkestone to catch the last ferry from there.

The conference was an awesome experience and so encouraging, if rather lacking in sleep as the sessions went on late into the night and the enthusiasm of some in our dormitory of nearly seven thousand to rise early in the morning and start praising God in song at 5am was not a good mixture for me.

During the event we helped to support Billy Graham at a crusade he was running in the Heysel Stadium in the city. Seeing hundreds of people going forward night after night to become Christians impacted me greatly. While queuing for lunch one day a thought drifted through my mind that I too was called to preach around the world to thousands of people. This notion caused me to laugh out loud and I dismissed it immediately as a daydream. The next day, while again queuing for lunch, another thought drifted through my mind: "One day you will be called on to lead the youth work at the church where you worship." Again I laughed because as far as I was concerned, our youth leader Bill was as near to God as anyone could be and I was never going to come close to comparing with him! So again I dismissed the thought as fanciful. The following day, again waiting patiently in a line for lunch, a third thought came to me; that on my return from the conference I would be asked to teach in Sunday school. This seemed more plausible to me than the previous thoughts but still didn't seem too likely.

So you can imagine my surprise when on my return home I entered church the following Sunday and the Sunday school superintendent Brian approached me and told me that they were having trouble with a group of older boys. They had, however, noticed that I had a unique gifting. Imagine my amazement at this – and so I enquired exactly what deeply spiritual gift they had recognised that I possessed. He calmly told me that he had observed that the young boys appeared to be frightened of me and they could use that to good effect with this group of lads! For once, my biker appearance qualified me for something: to teach Sunday school.

At that moment the thoughts that had visited me in Brussels drifted back through my mind. The same voice said, "See – you are going to teach Sunday school. Now believe Me that you will do all that I have said to you."

Yet again I quickly dismissed these thoughts as daydreams and once more laughed at my stupidity for even entertaining such notions. I got on with what I had been asked to do. I don't know who learnt more in those Sunday school classes – the boys or I!

As a new believer I was on a steep learning curve. I had noticed that Christians often heard God yet seemed to ignore what He was telling them to do. So I boldly announced to our youth leader, Bill, that within the next few years I intended to be the greatest man of God this world had ever seen, as I was not just going to hear what God was saying but would actually do what He told me immediately. I felt sure this would lead me to do great things for God.

Clearly I haven't become the greatest man of God this world has ever seen and hopefully I have learnt a few lessons in humility over the years! In that time, I have had a few disagreements with God but understand where Bob Mumford was coming from when he said that God had once declared to him, "Bob, you and I are incompatible and I don't change." This is a truth I too have learnt over the years. I still essentially believe that the secret to becoming everything that God intends you to be is simply hearing God and doing whatever He tells you as quickly as possible. The arguments only slow you down on the journey to fulfilling your destiny in God. We should all remember Jesus' mother's words to the servants at the wedding in Cana of Galilee: "Whatever He says to you, do it."[4]

Fear and disappointment have slowed my progress too often and at times stopped me altogether from doing what God has instructed. Fear of what other people might think, fear of getting things wrong, fear of failure and disappointments have also played their part, which is ridiculous. Why should the past stop us from stepping into all that God has for us?

Many years later, this was exampled to me when my smartphone was entering multiple appointments for events in my diary. I duly booked an appointment in Basingstoke with a technician to remedy the problem. He assured me that all my data would be backed up before he rebooted the system to correct the fault. I watched in dismay as my diary deleted all its entries, past, present and future. Kim, sitting at home, was also distraught to see all the data disappearing before her very eyes! Eventually it became apparent that we had permanently lost our diaries. The next week was spent trying to recall and reconstruct our future commitments. To this day we cannot be sure that we did not miss an appointment but nobody complained! This incidence reminded us that the past is unimportant; our focus should be on today and our future.

Failure and disappointments are merely the battle scars of people who are moving on with their God. We can clearly see this illustrated from the lives of biblical characters. Simon Peter denied knowing Jesus,[5] Gideon believed that his genealogy affected what he could do,[6]

---

[4] John 2:5 (NASB)
[5] See Mark 14
[6] See Judges 6:15-16

and Joseph, having heard God's word, was sold into slavery and later found himself in jail.[7]

Interestingly, success can also stop you moving on. This impacted me when I was asked by a young believer whom I had personally lead to the Lord some five years earlier if God had done anything new in my life since then. After metaphorically picking myself up off of the floor from what I perceived to be her cheek, I asked her what was behind her line of questioning. She replied, "It's just that all your stories are the same ones you were telling when I first got saved!"

I realised in that moment that the successes of the past were stopping me moving on into all God had for me in the present. The stories are great as they bring glory to God but we cannot afford to set up camp in the past whether it be around disappointment or success. We are called to a life of following Jesus, and to walk in that we need to keep moving forward. Paul writes to the church at Philippi, "Forgetting what is behind and straining toward what is ahead, I press on toward the goal to win the prize for which God has called me heavenward in Christ Jesus."[8] That is great advice that all of us should take! Every day is a fresh start with Jesus, who has a plan for our lives to give us a future and a hope.[9]

Another means the devil has used to stop me moving on is bringing me to a place of double-mindedness. He clouds the path ahead with an abundance of choices so we become confused, not sure which is the right one; one day thinking one direction is right, the next thinking something different. I realised that I was prone to being in this position. I recognised that I was not in the best of places but was paralysed by the thought of getting it wrong and ending up in a worse position. Yet the longer I stayed in this place, the direr things seemed to get. It seemed impossible to hear God and I became more and more confused. Then one day I read James 1:5-8 which talks about the double-minded man being unstable in all his ways, unable to receive anything from the Lord. As I read the scripture I realised in a moment that it was describing me and I knew my condition was why I was struggling to hear God in the way I usually did. I knew I needed to make a decision on a particular issue but was still not sure

---

[7] Genesis 37:28; 39:20
[8] Philippians 3:13-14
[9] See Jeremiah 29:11

which way to go, and then I heard God gently say, "Just go one way or the other. It doesn't matter which one you choose; you will at least become single-minded. Once you start moving, if you get it wrong, I can redirect you because it's easier to redirect a moving object. But if you stay double-minded you become unstable in all your ways and it is almost impossible to move on."

I learnt a great lesson that day. It is so important to keep moving on with God. It is not so important to get it right all the time; sometimes we just have to learn from our mistakes.

The disciples knew this only too well when they had been unable to heal the epileptic boy.[10] They came to Jesus privately after He had rebuked the demon and cast it out, asking why *they* could not cast it out. It is so important that we learn from our mistakes. There is nothing stopping us doing just what those early disciples did – coming to Jesus privately and asking why we were unable to do something or why things did not work out the way we thought they should have. Having talked with a few successful Christian leaders over the years, all of them are happy to admit that they have made a few mistakes along the way. The difference is that they have sought to learn from those mistakes rather than be dragged down by them or even give up on what the Bible teaches, a course of action which is always disastrous. My walk with God tells me that if we are seeking to be in a right relationship with Him, then even if we head off in completely the wrong direction, He can turn us around; the important thing is to keep moving. It bears repeating that we need to realise that disappointment and failures are the battle scars of a people who are seeking to press on with their God. It never ceases to amaze me the grace and patience that God extends towards me when I have found myself stationary because of fear, setbacks or enjoying triumphs. He is always ready with a simple question or a word of encouragement that once again gets me moving forward.

Sometime in my early years of faith I read the passage from Acts 3 in which Peter and John healed the man at the Beautiful Gate. I felt prompted that God wanted me also to minister to the sick and shared this with a close friend Martin from church. At that time only the elders prayed for the sick in our church, in line with James 5:14-15,

---

[10] See Mark 9:20-29

so an opportunity for this to happen seemed unlikely. However, the very next Sunday one of our leaders stood up in the meeting and announced that they had been asked to pray for a lady with a bad back but had felt God saying they should not minister to this lady as Father was wanting to use someone else to pray for her. We all waited to see whom this might be but no one responded to their request. So my friend stood up and announced that I had told him that I felt that God was calling me to pray for the sick. I was acutely embarrassed by this but went to the front and prayed for her. Nothing appeared to happen. For the following week I continued to pray for her each night. I contacted her and asked how she was but she did not immediately improve. Towards the end of my week of prayer she was able to declare that the longstanding pain she had been suffering from had gone and that she was completely pain-free. I was so pleased that God had answered my prayers for this lady!

CHAPTER FOUR

The Blessing of God

MY HUNGER FOR MORE OF GOD continued to grow and I started to visit a Youth With A Mission centre at Holmstead Manor, some fifty miles or so from my home town. Again I was exposed to young people who were sold out for God; I could not get enough of the teaching and bought study guides to work on when at home. Every time I met with other Christians, I would share the things that I was learning. There was a young lady who was also studying the same books and we agreed to meet together to learn which I really enjoyed. As the months of study went by we became the best of friends.

At some point I realised that this relationship had become more than just a friendship. I had fallen in love with her and asked her to marry me after first explaining that God had called me to be a preacher, something I wasn't sure could ever happen in my own strength but that I knew would happen if God opened the doors. I wasn't very romantic and had no money so simply asked her if she could lend me the money to buy a ring I had spotted in the jeweller's window we had just passed. Thank God that she didn't judge me on my proposal or we would have never gone any further in our relationship; instead she graciously lent me the money and accepted my proposal! I'm not even sure that I ever gave her the money back but one year later, in the July of 1979, we were married.

Shortly before the wedding I fell some thirty feet while working on the roof of our recently purchased house. Various 'wags' in my family assumed that I had stepped back to admire my work! I landed on the front garden, which consisted of a small patch of grass only three feet wide by five feet in length and surrounded by a brick wall and concrete paths. This was a miracle in itself as landing anywhere else in the garden would have certainly caused me more serious injuries.

The fall resulted in me taking a trip to the hospital in an ambulance with all sirens and lights blazing. Praise God, I had not broken any bones, but I was kept in overnight for observation. This extended to a few days as each time the nurses got me out of bed to try to get me walking, I would black out and wake up back in the bed with a few more bruises. Eventually I became stable enough to be discharged but only then did I realise how much support I was getting in hospital and how hospitals are set up with furniture at the correct height to minimise the need to bend and twist when moving around.

The day I was discharged from hospital, Kim took me home to my parents' house, but sadly the muscles in my back had seized up while sitting in the car and I was unable to get out of the vehicle. At one point I thought that I would have to return back to the hospital! With a lot of help, causing me considerable pain, I was extracted from the car. Once in the house my mother, who had been a nurse, suggested that a warm bath might help loosen my back muscles, and so a bath was run and I was helped to the downstairs bathroom and encouraged to get undressed. This whole process took the best part of fifteen minutes before I was lying in the warm water, but the expected relief from discomfort did not come and instead the pain of the muscles relaxing was far greater than anything I had experienced up until that point. This motivated me to get up and out of the bath in all of twenty seconds. "Best left for another day!" I thought. Praise God, I did recover, although I was left in near constant pain in my lower back. Over the ensuing few months my GP tried to help by prescribing ever stronger painkillers, until one day he told me that I would just have to learn to live with the situation. Pain Clinics were a thing of the future!

For two years I coped with the pain, popping pills when it got too much. One day while at a friend's house I was taking some pills and she asked what they were and how long I had been on them. On hearing my reply, she declared that I should never have been allowed to take these pills for so long and told me to stop taking them right away as they were highly addictive. I remember feeling let down by my doctor and declaring that I would never take a pill again!

Shortly after this I was in a meeting listening to Ian Andrews, a man with a great healing ministry. During his preaching he paused and declared that there was someone in the room who was in constant pain with damaged kidneys and God wanted to heal them. No one responded and Ian then went on to say that this person was in constant pain and, indeed, was in pain at that very moment. Still no one responded. I thought to myself, "I wish he would have a word for someone who has damaged their back and is in constant pain!" as I was sitting there in agony. Finally, Ian declared that God had told him that the person had had a fall and been told that they had damaged their back but that God had revealed to Ian that it was not their back but in fact their kidneys. At this point I realised he was talking about me and so I went forward for him to pray for me. When I got to the front of the hall, Ian called someone else over to pray for me, a person whom I had little respect for because of things I had heard them say. I was so disappointed that I very nearly missed out on what God wanted to do for me but just in time I remembered that it is God who is the healer, not man, and I put my trust in Him and His ability to heal me no matter who was praying for me. I walked out of that room pain-free and have never had a day's pain from my kidneys since.

Our first house was a wonderful provision and was more than we could ever have hoped for. It was, however, in quite a dilapidated state having been rented out as two flats for about twenty years with very little maintenance carried out. We were so blessed by the army of family and friends who gave so freely of their time to come and help us clean and renovate the Victorian 'semi'; wiring was replaced, walls were taken down, the kitchen was replaced, the window frames were stripped and repainted, all with their help. This enabled us to open the home up and regularly have young people and others around to enjoy it with us.

To own a home of our own was a miracle in itself as it was beyond our wildest dreams – our God is so good! We had saved every spare penny for the whole year since getting engaged to enable us to have a deposit and He had miraculously provided the house to buy. This Victorian semi was only being advertised by a postcard in the corner of its front window and was priced well below the market rate due to avoidance of inheritance taxes. Even in this we saw Him move to bless us again and again. During the renovation, I returned home one day to find Kim crying while painting the kitchen units which were old, mouldy and falling to bits. Her tears touched me and as I comforted her, we prayed to God for a better kitchen. Within a couple of days, we had been given a small gift, nowhere near enough to buy a new kitchen but we started to look for a second-hand one after we had tithed the money. Soon a friend told us that there was a lady who had just moved into a brand new house in the next town. The new home owner did not like the kitchen and, as she had had it removed and a new one put in, now wanted to sell this unused kitchen. We went to see it and offered her the money we had been given; she accepted our offer and also included a refrigerator with the units. The units fitted our kitchen perfectly and we learnt that God is able to give you far more than you could ever expect as long as you are seeking first His kingdom and His righteousness.[11]

A great help and encouragement were our next door neighbours, Peter and Mary. I had been friends with them since soon after coming into the church. Many are the times that I spent around the kitchen table with them discussing spiritual truths. Moving into the house next door to them meant that these times were more frequent and some years in the future Peter and I formed a partnership as he invited me to join his building company. What followed was a steep learning curve as in the first week that I joined him we were tasked to dig out and lay a new concrete drive. I returned each evening exhausted and in pain and seriously questioned whether I had done the right thing in this change of career!

As tight as money was in those early days of our marriage, we determined that we would always seek to give the first fruits of whatever we had back to God and as a result the house was fully furnished on an extremely low budget as things just seemed to flow to our door. So much so that one day we were invited out to dinner by a

---

[11] See Matthew 6:33

financially well off couple in the church whom we hardly knew. They were both doctors and on very good salaries. Halfway through the meal, just before the dessert was served, the wife asked a very direct question: "Can you tell me, do you tithe your income?" The enquiry came out of the blue and we answered yes, at which point she turned on her husband and blurted out, "I told you that they must!" It transpired that this couple had been observing us since we had been married, had seen how blessed we were and had been discussing how we could manage to live so well on our lower incomes. She had told her husband that we must tithe to which he replied, "They can't afford to do that; how could they possibly do it?"

That night we learnt again that God's economy didn't require you to be earning huge sums of money for Him to bless you in ways that were clear to all those around you and that tithing wasn't something you could afford to do, it was something you cannot afford not to do! The Bible teaches us to, "Give, and it will be given to you [in] good measure, pressed down, shaken together and running over..."[12] God wants us as His people to have generous natures just like Him. He is just so good!

My giving did get us into trouble occasionally and one day when our bank statement arrived I discovered that we were several thousands of pounds overdrawn. I did not understand why this had come about as God had always provided for our needs and so I had not really kept a close eye on the bank balance.

When I talked to God about it He cautioned me that just because I saw a need, it didn't mean that He had called me to meet that need. We must be led by the Spirit in every area of our lives.[13] I apologised and asked Him to help me out of the problem. There was, at that time, a particular job that had a far higher profit margin than any other work I was undertaking. I asked Father to give me more of those jobs than I normally got. He answered wonderfully and where I would normally only get one or two of these jobs a year, within the next few weeks I was asked to quote for ten and was invited to complete nine of them which meant that within two months we were back in credit. I had worked hard to earn the money but God had provided the work to enable me to get out of debt.

---

[12] Luke 6:38a
[13] See Galatians 5:22

CHAPTER FIVE

A Taste of Things to Come

WE HAD BEEN MARRIED FOR just over a year when the opportunity came to be part of a team travelling to Sri Lanka to encourage a group of churches there. A number of our ministers had travelled to India in the preceding years ministering at conferences and to churches in the south of the country. Some pastors from Sri Lanka had attended these events and the leadership decided that it was a good time to see how they were implementing the teaching. I had asked previously if I might be able to join the pastors when they travelled to India but those going did not think this was appropriate. Now here was the opportunity I had longed for.

I was overjoyed at this and both Kim and I believed it was the right thing to do. Although we could manage the cost of the trip, it did mean that we chose to go without a lot of the things newly married couples hope to get in the early years of marriage – but God is no man's debtor.[14] In the early eighties Sri Lanka was not the holiday destination that it is now and it took over twenty-two hours by plane to get there. When we arrived in Colombo the team picked up their bags and left the airport to meet the pastor, who was eagerly waiting outside to meet us. Nothing could prepare me for what I was about to experience: the sights, the sounds, the smells and the temperature!

---

[14] See Psalm 37:25

Thousands of people were moving in every direction by foot, on ox carts, bicycles, and by cars and buses that were at least fifty years old. They carried every imaginable thing with them from chickens and pigs to beds and chairs. People were grabbing us and begging for money. Others wanted to buy our watches while yet others wanted to buy the jeans we were wearing. Some wanted to sell us goods, others wanted to carry our bags for us. Naively we gave our bags to a couple of young men only to see them disappear from sight, but fortunately the pastor who was waiting for us saw what happened; he and his team gave chase, and our bags and possessions were recovered.

Our first night was spent at the YWCA[15] which, considering we were five young *men*, was interesting! We were booked to speak at churches all over the island and would be transported around by car, coach, train and ox cart, all of which looked as if they belonged in a museum. It really was an adventure. Everywhere we went people were glad to meet us and would listen as we taught from God's Word and shared our testimonies. Accommodation varied greatly from very poor hotels to barns to the equivalent of a Salvation Army doss house where we were all eaten alive by bed bugs.

One day while walking through a market, I noticed that some of the meat on sale was rotten, green and festering and pointed this out to one of the other team members. We watched in amazement as someone purchased a piece of it. That night as we sat down to dinner, we realized that the man who was cooking the meal was the same fellow we had seen buy the meat in the market. This was too much for my team mate John! As soon as he reluctantly put the meat in his mouth, his face started to change colour, which was quickly followed by him being violently sick. All the other team mates with one accord shouted, "Praise God!" as before we had left England it had been prophesied over us that one of us would be ill. Four of us rejoiced that we were not the ones to suffer. Such sensitivity for the suffering of our hapless teammate! It is not the sort of encouraging word that you want to hear when you are heading so far from home but – bless God! – it was the only time any of us were sick and we were all in good health for the rest of the trip.

---

[15] Young Women's Christian Association

The organised gatherings were great but some of the spontaneous meetings were even better. We had been for an early morning swim in the Indian Ocean near to where we were staying. The fishermen were packing up their boats and washing their nets from the previous night's fishing. They seemed very interested in us as in those days they rarely would encounter a white face and here were five young men swimming in the sea. I was encouraged by our team leader Bill to preach the Gospel to these men. So standing on the back of an upturned boat I shared the Good News of Jesus Christ with around twenty fishermen, and a number of them gave their lives to Jesus there on the beach. Another day we were taken to see the fish market, which was an auction of the previous night's catch, and our presence brought the whole proceedings to a halt. Eventually we were invited to the podium and asked to share. Again one of us preached the Good News and again people got saved. What a thrill these impromptu meetings were! I imagined it was much the same in biblical times on the shores of the Lake of Galilee.

One morning we had a report that there was Tamil Tiger activity around Kilinochchi. The terrorist group, some five to ten thousand strong, was formed in the mid-seventies and was actively engaged in violent offensives to force the government to form a separate state for the Tamils in the northern part of the island. We were scheduled to visit the next day and it was decided that we should not attempt to travel to that region due to Bill's reluctance to expose the younger members of the team to danger. I think he was wondering how he might explain such an action to the parents if their sons ended up dead in a ditch!

That night I slept fitfully and woke feeling sure that I should go even if the rest of the team did not. I shared my feelings with Bill and it was agreed that two of us would go. So John and I were dropped at the side of the road and were met by the pastor who had brought sedan chairs to carry us through the jungle! Naturally we refused such ostentation and walked alongside everyone else. It took at least an hour to travel the jungle path to the village and when we arrived we were enthusiastically welcomed by the church. We preached, shared testimonies and again people got saved. We even prayed for a few sick people and saw them healed.

I was asked to bless a baby, who promptly blessed me back all over my shirt. The shirt was taken away to be washed at the river and so we stopped on for a meal. By the time we came to leave, night had fallen and we now had to walk through the jungle in the pitch black as there was no ambient light with the cover of the trees above occluding the light from the moon and stars.

As we made our way, our guide regaled us with various horror stories. At one point, as we came to a clearing, our guide Joseph declared, "Brother Tim, we used to have a village here in this clearing but one night a herd of wild elephants came running through the village flattening the houses and trampling a number of our people to death!" After that, every branch cracking or strange noise emanating from the dark jungle filled me with thoughts of wild elephants stampeding towards us in the dark.

A little farther on Joseph told us, "Brother Tim, Pastor Gomez was coming to preach in our village last year and just here was bitten by a most venomous snake. He rebuked it in Jesus' name, continued to our village, preached the Gospel and then he dropped down dead!" I understand that the snake will usually kill within a short period of time but Pastor Gomez' faith saw him through to the end of his preaching engagement – but this was little comfort as I did not want my faith to be tested as to how long I might survive a bite! Every twig that we stepped on now potentially became a lethal serpent that could shorten our lives dramatically! The jungle, which had seemed such a nice place as we had walked to the village that afternoon, was now threatening and ominous terrain.

When we eventually got back to the road we discovered that there were no buses running and so we had to walk some miles until we found a place where a number of vehicles were parked for the night. We managed to persuade one bus driver to take us on to Jaffna where we were to reconnect with the rest of the team. After much bartering we agreed to pay what he would earn for such a trip during the daytime but that we would stop and pick people up along the way and charge them to come on our bus to offset the expense. We set off on our way – and headlong into a frightening ordeal.

No buses were allowed on the road at that time of night because the Tigers had imposed a curfew and no one was meant to be travelling after dark. You can imagine the trouble we were in when we came to a road block manned by a number of Tamil Tiger teenagers with AK47s. Everyone was made to get off the bus and it was quite clear we were getting the blame for breaking the curfew. They thought that we might be supporters of the government, a number of whom had been murdered by the guerrillas in the area just a few days beforehand. The situation was deteriorating by the minute until an older guy who seemed to be in charge of these teenagers walked up to see what was going on. He asked to see our passports and as soon as he saw the blue of our British documents (as they were in those days before the nondescript reddish pink of today's passports) everything appeared to get a lot friendlier. The Tigers became more relaxed and their guns were lowered. It appeared that the leader had worked with the British at some point in his past and had a lot of respect for us as a nation and so we were let through and allowed to complete our journey with much relief on our part!

We eventually met up with the rest of the team and although we were several hours late we actually made a profit on our deal with the bus driver as there were more people breaking the curfew than he had obviously expected! The team back in Jaffna were sure by this time that we had indeed been kidnapped by the Tigers and were now lying dead in a ditch somewhere. It was fantastic to experience God's protection in this way having responded to His leading to travel out to the village.

On another occasion we walked into a remote village and everyone started to treat us very strangely. Our leader Bill and I were taken to see the head man and we sat on the floor talking with him. My skin had tanned very brown in the hot Sri Lankan sun and my blond hair had been bleached to almost white. Although only twenty-two years of age, this combination had led the people to believe that I was one of their gods come down to earth. They thought that my white hair was a sign of age yet I appeared to be young and my deep tan had convinced them I was not Caucasian. The only conclusion to be made was that I was indeed a god made flesh and they took some convincing that this was not the case! We understood how the apostle Paul must have felt when he resorted to tearing his clothes to prove he was a mere mortal.[16] Bill, as the mission leader, was a little put out

---

[16] See Acts 14:14

that they considered him to be a simple man travelling with a higher being!

We went on to travel from Sri Lanka by paddle steamer to southern India. We had queued for some thirty-six hours on the dock as the Tamils leaving the country were being given priority by the authorities. This persecuted group were leaving in droves looking for peace and security from the hostilities they were subject to on this beautiful but trouble-torn island. During this wait we booked into a hotel which was made up of what can only be described as very poor garden sheds made from palm leaves. The toilet was the beach and when the lights went out at night the rats came out to play and were running around and over our beds. In the dark, one team member cried out, "I've been bitten! Find the torch!" My response was one of extreme reluctance to put my feet on the ground among the frolicking vermin but one of the other team members was far braver and jumped up to find a torch and shed some light on the situation. What had felt like a bite in the dark to an overexcited imagination was in fact a burn from a smouldering wick designed to repel mosquitoes which a rat had dislodged from the shelf above our heads and which had then fallen onto my friend's arm. Only one of us, John, seemed to get any sleep that night and he was oblivious to the rats eating the bananas perched on his pillow – which was just as well!

Praise God, the next day we managed to get passage on the ferry, which appeared to be a relic left over from the days of the British Raj. We played our part by sitting on the deck in rattan chairs and thought back to a very different period in history. The first glimpse we had of our destination from out at sea was the Hindu temple at Rameshwaram, which dominated the skyline of an otherwise low rise town. Upon arrival our cases were thrown from the ship onto a flotilla of little boats that took them ashore. We were reunited with them at customs where the officials insisted on searching our cases at least three times each. Eventually we were allowed through and spent a few days there ministering with Body of Christ Ministries led by Moses Paulose. In the following years this ministry has expanded phenomenally and planted churches throughout this region and has also established a Bible school.

Rameshwaram is one of the most holy places in India for Hindus and we were encouraged to live and act in a way that was sympathetic to the local traditions. While with this ministry, we slept on concrete floors on rush mats with straw pillows. Mealtimes took place without any form of cutlery and we ate our curry and rice with our hands just as the locals did. If the curry (which we had for breakfast, dinner and tea) was hot then it would burn our soft Western fingers and, if it was hot with chilli, our stomachs and our bottoms when it eventually finished its course through our bodies!

Everything we experienced in this town was so different to what we were used to. The Hindu temple dominated the town and was never out of view, reminding those who worshipped there of the statues within it which seemed to be designed to scare the adherents into worship of their gods or suffer a terrible fate. Just being in the town you could feel the oppression, and the temperature had risen significantly on arriving in India and we were all finding this extra heat very difficult. One day while walking with the pastor praying through an area of the town, a number of us succumbed to the heat and had to be taken into a small house to rest. The temperature was over forty degrees Celsius.

We came across a poor cow that had been hit by a car and one of its legs was just hanging on by a small piece of skin. The animal was clearly in pain and infection had set in to the open wound but when I suggested that we put it out of its misery, I was told that if I did that the people would certainly kill me as this was a holy animal and nothing could be done to it. Consequently, the cow was left to die a slow, painful death.

The next part of our journey involved embarking on the overnight steam train to Madras, which reminded me very much of various travel shows I had watched, especially Michael Palin's Great Train Journeys. The scenery to be seen was truly stunning and lent insight into rural Southern India.

The train was left over from the British occupation and the passage was a truly amazing experience. At one station along the route a group of waiters came on and took our orders for dinner, but before they could deliver the food the train moved on, much to our dismay and confusion. About an hour later we pulled into the next station and a second group of waiters delivered our food, each meal to the correct person. We had failed to realise that the orders were telegraphed up the line so the food would be prepared ready for when we arrived, a marvellous system!

Again we were well received by the churches in Madras and saw many people healed, saved and added to the church. All too soon our time there was over and we found ourselves at Madras International Airport[17] ready to embark on the twenty-two-hour journey back home to England. Or so we thought!

Sitting in the departure lounge we were called to the desk and told that there were no seats available for us on the flight. This was a mystery as we had confirmed tickets. It transpired that bribes had been paid by people with unconfirmed tickets and that they were now occupying our seats on the aircraft.

After a heated discussion with the airport staff, a manager was called and tasked with sorting out the problem. We watched through the windows as he walked across the tarmac, entered the plane and several minutes later people with their hand luggage were unceremoniously ejected from the plane and thrown onto the tarmac below! We were then informed by said manager that the problem had been rectified and our five seats were now ready for us. Once again we realised the power of a British passport in this part of the world at that time.

South East Asia had won my heart and I knew that I had unfinished business there. It would, however, be another ten years before I would return as God had work to do in me before I was ready to visit there again.

---

[17] now Chennai

CHAPTER SIX

First Steps

BACK IN THE UK, I FELT GOD encouraging me to apply for promotion at work and so I put my name forward for a job that was being advertised and was duly invited for an interview. I arrived at the appointed time and place to discover that one of the regional managers had decided to sit in on the interviews alongside my direct boss, which was a departure from the norm. My boss and I had fallen out sometime before due to my outspoken nature as a headstrong young man prior to my becoming a Christian and to say that he felt some measure of antipathy towards me is to put it mildly! I subsequently discovered that he had informed the panel that it was a waste of time interviewing me as there was no way I was suitable for promotion. However, such was the strength of the union that management was required to see all who applied. What my boss hadn't realised was that I was a changed man! I flew through the interview answering all the questions well and making a really good impression.

Later that day I was called back to the depot and into my boss's office. He demanded to know what had happened to me. He explained what he had said to the panel and how he had been made to look rather foolish in front of a regional manager. I explained that I had become a Christian and that was why I wanted the job, because I felt that God was urging me to do better things with my life. He informed me that I was considered to be too young for the position at this point but when the next opportunity should arise the regional manager had told the panel that I should be given the job. True to their word, the next promotion was mine. I am sure that God had prompted the regional manager to sit in on the interviews that day as, no doubt, I would not have been considered for the job due to my strained history with my boss. To be honest, I felt a little sorry for my boss as he had just not had any contact with me since I was saved and so was working with an old impression of me.

A week after we had returned from our honeymoon, our pastor Mike Pusey had visited us in our home and asked if we would be willing to lead the youth work in the church, which we were more than pleased to take on. That night the thought returned once more: "I have called you to preach to thousands around the world." But this time I didn't laugh – instead a light was kindled somewhere deep in my spirit, the light of faith that would grow to believe that God was able to do whatever He said.

Our work with the young people continued for several years and we found great joy in encouraging the youngsters in their faith just as we had been encouraged in ours during our time under Bill and Sue's wing. Our group grew both in numbers and in faith and we saw the teenagers take many great steps of faith.

It was a mixture of both fun and faith activities. We had weekends away camping in the New Forest and indoor camping with a church in Chichester, which gave the youngsters great scope for practical jokes, from the girls cling-filming the boys' toilet at night to ambushing me with flour and water on my birthday! We took advantage of a heavy snowfall – rare in those days – to go sledging one Sunday afternoon on the King George V playing fields in Farnborough. Then back to our house where we all steamed away nicely while we tumble-dried their clothes; boys downstairs, girls upstairs and me patrolling the stairs in between!

The group's faith really started to grow. They began to see each other's ailments healed and were invited into local schools to share their faith and minister to the children.

During this time God continued to challenge me about faith for healing both in my own life and in the lives of those we ministered to. It seemed to me that a key to ministering successfully to others was to be trusting God for healing in my own life. So I set about looking to

Him for healing no matter what sickness came my way, from stomach problems to headaches and even a suspected broken arm where you could feel the bones moving in ways they should not! They were all presented to God for His healing touch, and when my own faith did not bring deliverance from the symptoms, I would call for the elders of the church and have them pray for me. I would then trust God for the healing and would return to work whether I felt better or not. It never took more than an hour or two before receiving complete relief. I found my faith grew and my relationship with God deepened.

I noticed from looking at the life of Jesus that He did not often pray for people. When He ministered to them, He appeared to move in three main ways: He recognised their faith, instructed them to take some action or took some action Himself. Examples of these would be the centurion whom Jesus recognised possessed faith,[18] the lepers whom He instructed to show themselves to the priest,[19] and the account of where Jesus Himself rubbed mud into the blind man's eyes.[20] Indeed, when Jesus sent His disciples out, He commanded them to "heal the sick" – He did not tell them to "pray for the sick". In fact, the only context I can find in Scripture where we are called to pray for the sick is within the church.[21] I have realised that often we end up asking God to do something that He has already given us the authority to do ourselves, and why would He do something that He has commanded us to do? We need to recognise what we have been commissioned to do, and seek to build our faith to the place where we believe what God has declared and boldly take authority in the Name of Jesus and heal the sick, raise the dead and cast out demons, all the while declaring that the Kingdom of God is at hand.[22]

When I was confronted with sickness, I resolved to follow this model. For example, when I was on an outreach event in the town of Kettering in the Midlands during the eighties, I was sharing with some young teenagers on the street about how God healed and they

---

[18] See Matthew 8:13
[19] See Luke 17:14
[20] See John 9:6
[21] See James 5:14
[22] See Matthew 10:7-8

asked if I really believed God could heal today, to which I boldly declared, "Of course I do!"

One young man looked me in the face and ordered me to stay where I was while he went away and got his friend. He returned a few minutes later with another boy in tow and said, "OK, heal him!" It turned out this boy suffered with severe asthma so much so that he could not run or even walk at pace without having an attack. On a number of occasions at school an ambulance had been summoned to take him to hospital when he had tried to join in with the playground games. Now here was this young man with his friend, demanding that my God heal him.

As I prayed there in the shopping precinct, I felt God tell me to get the boy to run the length of the street. As I explained this to him, the other boys gathered around and informed me that I had better be ready to call the ambulance! Praise God, the sick lad agreed to run and set off jogging down the street. Immediately I felt God say, "He's not running and he will not be healed unless he runs." So at the top of my voice I shouted, "I told you to run. Now, run!" The boy shot off like the devil himself was chasing after him and returned from the other end of the street just as fast. He was winded and we all watched as he stood trying to regain his breath. As he did so, his face broke into the widest of smiles as there was no sign of an asthma attack. That night all the boys were in the meeting trying to find out more about the God who had healed their friend.

On my return home, one of our young people phoned to ask me to go round to pray for her as she was suffering with gastroenteritis and was feeling very weak. As we talked on the phone, God told me to tell her to be in church the next morning as she would be healed then.

The next day there was a powerful anointing for healing in the meeting, something that was still new and exciting to us in those days, with words of knowledge and people being healed in every corner. Yet my friend did not come forward so when we had finished praying for all the people I went to her and asked if she was still sick. She replied that she was, so we prayed. Immediately she was 'slain in the Spirit' and a few minutes later recovered and stood up pain-free and no longer feeling nauseous. Later she reported back to me that all signs of the sickness had gone and she was feeling well in herself again. You see, God responded to her faith; she got out of her sick bed and came to the meeting and He healed her.

It seemed at this time that the enemy did not like what was going on in the church and during one evening service there were lots of disturbances. I felt God call me to pray quietly against the enemy, binding his works amongst us. This I did throughout the remainder of the meeting and everything ran smoothly from then on. I thought nothing more of this, and the meeting finished and Kim and I started to walk home. Both of us had a sense that we were being followed but on looking behind us we could see no one there. We arrived home, went to bed and fell asleep without giving it any more thought.

That was until we both awoke with a start to see a dark figure dressed in a black cowl with the hood pulled over her head walking around our bedroom. Although this might sound as if it should have been a very disturbing incident, God gave us a great sense of peace because we knew it could do us no harm. We watched her walk around our bed and out of the door which she pulled to, and then she opened it again and put her head in and looked around before finally leaving and closing the door shut. Both Kim and I were surprised by this visitation. Clearly the demon which God had me bind during the meeting had followed us home, perhaps seeking to frighten us or even to do us harm. Throughout the experience we had felt God's presence protecting us, realising the truth of that passage that, "If God is for us who can be against us?"[23] and, "...greater is He who is in you than he who is in the world."[24] We prayed, and turned over and went back to sleep. From this point on I realised that the devil is truly defeated and we are called to plunder his goods,[25] and that we must fulfil that calling despite the enemy's attempts to distract and dissuade us.

---

[23] Romans 8:31b
[24] 1 John 4:4b (NASB)
[25] See Matthew 12:29

CHAPTER SEVEN

The Vision Unfolds

WE HAD BEEN WORKING SUCCESSFULLY with the young people in the Farnborough congregation but now the elder overseeing youth ministry in the work decided to amalgamate our group with the smaller group meeting in Cove. This change, although we did not initially welcome it, enabled us to step back and reassess which direction we should be heading in.

To that end the church were planning to plant a new congregation in Pinewood Village, a few miles from where we lived, and we felt God calling us to join the people who lived in that area and help them in their new venture. Our house was sold and we started to look for a new one there but were unable to find anything we liked. This became a real problem and we started to question if we should indeed be moving to that village, yet we knew that God had said, "Go!"

We shared this with some friends and prayed together about the situation. During this time God spoke to them and told them that the next day an estate agent's envelope would arrive at our house with the details of the house we were to buy. Sure enough, the following morning the agent sent us just one set of details. They were of a house that we had viewed some time before and had dismissed. However, we could not remember why we had rejected the house and without viewing it again made an offer, which was accepted. Shortly after, we moved into this, our new home, on the Westfield estate in Cove.

After settling in we were asked to lead one of the home groups in the area, an offer which we declined as I knew that God had called me to be an evangelist and not into pastoral ministry. I told the leaders that I felt sure that if I took on a home group, there would shortly be no one left in it because I would tell people just what I thought and at times that would not be very shepherd-like!

However, within a few months we were asked to reconsider. This time I felt God impress upon me that we just needed to serve this new work in whatever way our leaders needed us to. Sure enough there were times when I told the group the way I saw things with all honesty but to my amazement the people responded positively and the group started to grow in numbers to the point where we were now looking after two groups both of which were growing. God was causing this new church to prosper.

My gifting was also growing and I was given opportunities to preach under the guidance of my pastor, Bob. On the first opportunity, I woke up that morning with stomach cramps, feeling dizzy and sick. I wondered if I was suffering from food poisoning because I was not by now of a nervous disposition; God had built my confidence in public speaking. I arrived at church and had to visit the toilet twice to be sick during the worship. I got up to preach and pray for people afterwards and then returned to the toilet to be sick again! Despite this, I had a sense that I had started to fulfil what God had told me back in Brussels all those years before.

At this time, we met regularly in regional celebrations in Cove Secondary School. These were great times when all of our churches in the area came together to worship and praise God. Once I was at the front of the hall praying for people and I turned to see Kim. I heard God tell me that my wife was pregnant and that this time everything would be fine. Her first pregnancy had ended in a traumatic miscarriage after four months which had deeply affected us both. Nine months to that day Rebekah was born – on Christmas Day 1982, a day which will always be remembered in our house as a time of God's blessing. Becky was, and still is, a beautiful daughter and has been a great joy to us with a generous nature. We are both very proud of all she is and all she has achieved.

With everything else that was going on, I felt God was encouraging me to step out in faith and start my own plumbing and gas maintenance business so that I might be able to release more time into the Kingdom. On the launch day, as we had no work booked, I went out delivering leaflets advertising the firm through the doors of the houses in the village. On my return home the phone started to ring; the bookings flowed in and we were never short of work.

The business ran for some ten years until eventually I had to give it up to enable me to work full time in the ministry – something I had always declared I already did; it was just that I had a job as well! We need to realise that we are all called to be 'full time' for God wherever we are, whatever we are doing. Everything that we are involved in during our daily lives should be seen as being spiritual and an act of service to Him. We are here to be light in the darkness, a beacon at the entrance to a safe haven.[26]

Some years ago my son Thomas (who was eight years old at the time) and I joined some other fathers and sons for a sailing weekend. Our original plan was to sail down from the Hamble, past the Isle of Wight and on to the Channel Islands for the weekend. Sadly, the weather was not all that we had hoped for and we found ourselves in a force eight gale in the English Channel, sailing close to the Isle of Wight. This was a scary experience for novice sailors! That first night our efforts were focused on comforting some very seasick small boys.

As we sailed past the Needles lighthouse we saw the green and red beacons illuminating the entrance to Poole Harbour. What a blessed relief to know that a safe haven was such a short distance away! When Jesus uses the analogy, "You are the light of the world," this is what we're meant to be; an invitation to all those in trouble on the rough seas of this world to enter the safe haven of the Kingdom of God.

From the outset of Gold Star Gas Maintenance, we felt that one of the reasons for the business' existence was to bless the church and to be able to serve God. Consequently, we decided that we would tithe my time as well as our money. I told the leaders that I would give one day a week of my time to the church to use in whatever way they saw fit. I would photocopy in the office, babysit, decorate for single parents, run errands, in fact anything and everything I was

---

[26] See Matthew 5:14

asked to do. None of this seemed very spiritual to me at the time but I felt God say that it was important to learn to serve.

The church had continued to grow throughout the region, planting new works such as the one we were part of in Cove. We sought to meet together once a month, thus confirming our regional identity, but we found it increasingly difficult to find a venue that was large enough for us all to gather in. To this end it was suggested by our leaders that we should purchase an old cinema in Aldershot to turn into a meeting place for the regional work. This was accepted with great enthusiasm and we all started to pray as to how much we should give to the project to enable it to happen. People sold cars and gave the money to the project; ladies who did not need to work took on jobs for a period of time and gave what they earned. Everyone did whatever they thought God was telling them to do to see the vision fulfilled.

Kim and I prayed independently to find out from God what our faith contribution should be and we set a target date for an answer. In matters of finance we have always sought God to be in agreement with each other regarding how much and where our giving should be directed. Agreement is a powerful thing, releasing God's blessing. And when we have a three-way agreement – God, husband and wife – nothing is impossible to us.[27]

On the appointed day, I returned home to find Kim on her knees spring cleaning, with her head deep in a kitchen cupboard. I asked whether she had been given a figure by God to which she answered in the affirmative and asked if I had too, which I had.

On asking her what that figure was, she said, "No, you go first!" I mentioned the number that I felt God had told me, which was about a third of the value of our house at that time. I watched as Kim jumped up with a start and banged her head on the cupboard shelf, amazed that God had given us both the same figure, a sum that was way beyond what we were able to earn or raise in any way other than selling our house.

After much prayer we put our home on the market and the house duly sold. Kim was expecting our second child and, by the time the sale had gone through, was six months into the pregnancy. Although

---

[27] See Ecclesiastes 4:12 and Matthew 18:19-20

the equity in the house more than covered what we felt God had told us to give, having given it there was not enough left for a deposit on any sort of accommodation. Yet during the period of time it took for the sale to complete, we felt God encouraging us that He would give us another home of our own. We had received several prophecies encouraging us to put our trust in Him.

To this end we refused to even look at renting a house, declaring that God was going to provide. The day of our move came and with the help of many friends we moved all of our belongings out of the house into the removal truck. We still had nowhere to go. We didn't understand why the house God had promised had not turned up but we decided we would not give up on Him. Friends offered for us to stay in their spare room so our possessions were distributed around the garages and spare rooms of members of the church as we moved into the one room at Chris and Bernadette's home.

This was a difficult time in many ways, the worst of which for me was when we went to visit my parents; my father, who was not a believer, told me that Kim and Becky were always welcome to come and visit but he never wanted to see me again as no son of his could ever have made his family homeless. This was a real low point for me but, praise God, there were also high points during this time as well.

One night we woke in the early hours of the morning to see Becky, who was just over two years old, sitting up in her cot at the bottom of our bed looking intently up at the windowsill with an odd look on her face. When I asked her, "What are you looking at, darling?" she replied, "Can't you see the silver man watching us, Daddy? He's sitting on the window sill." I had to admit that no, I couldn't, but it encouraged Kim and I that God knew where we were and had sent His angels to watch over our little family.

During this time, we were given a word from God through Bob, saying that we were released from a commitment no one knew we had made to living in the village. Little did he know the impact that word would have on us. We lived with our friends for two months until a couple in Ash – Alan and Doreen – offered us the use of their house while they were on holiday for a fortnight. They told us that if we were still homeless on their return, we were welcome to stay on with them.

During our month with them God started to release money to us totalling some two-and-a-half times that which we had given. Some came in directly and also God had spoken to someone in the church who, like us, was also moving house at that time. Father asked them to significantly reduce the price of their house which enabled us to purchase the property as our new home. It was much larger than our previous house and in a more upmarket area.

We moved in just one week before our second child, Thomas, was born in June of 1985. God is faithful! Tom was a great boy who has grown into a wonderful young man and is now in ministry. We had given sacrificially towards the purchase of the new church building and God had given us so much more back. You can never out-give our God! My earthly father came round to see our new home shortly after we moved in and asked how we could possibly afford to buy such a nice home. When I explained to him, he demanded that I give the money back, but not knowing where much of it had come from that was not possible and so we never spoke of it again. Kingdom economics are rather unique! Sometime later Dad told me that he was so proud of all that I had become.

Having moved from the congregation where we had taken an active role in its leadership, we now found ourselves in a congregation with an already established leadership team and there seemed no apparent role for us to play. But God had other ideas.

CHAPTER EIGHT

Learning to Trust God

WE WERE CALLED ON TO BE INVOLVED with one of the main leaders, Mike, to help with another church plant. Our other main leader, Derek Brown, asked me to travel with him on the one day a week we were still giving to the church. This was 'on the job' training in a way, which was perfect for me as I had not thrived academically while at school.

My business was still prospering, providing all we needed even though I was only giving it three or four days a week by this time. But even through my business God was teaching us to trust Him in increasingly deeper ways. One morning we received a call from our bank manager asking me to come in and see him. When I entered his office he handed me a cheque that I had banked which was payment for a large job we had just completed. It represented over a week's work plus nearly a thousand pounds worth of materials which I had installed. My bank manager informed me that the cheque had not been honoured by the bank it was being drawn against and he had presented it three times. His counterpart had eventually informed him that there was no money in this account and never had been at any time anywhere near enough to cover the cheque. My bank manager returned the cheque to me and encouraged me to take legal advice.

My business adviser told me that I should take the couple to court and reclaim my costs through them. My solicitor advised me that a fraud could have been committed as the couple had knowingly issued a cheque without the funds to cover it. He directed me to take advice from the police. None of these courses of action sat well in my spirit. God reminded me of the passage I had read in my Bible that morning which said, "...my God will supply all your needs according to His riches in glory..."[28]

Father asked me, "Do you believe what you have read?"

"Of course I do!" I replied. "It's Your Word."

He continued, "Who gives you the money to live – the people you worked for or Me?"

I answered, "Well, ultimately it's You, God, who gives us the money."

Father instructed me, "Then write to this couple and tell them that you realize they have no money and that you are a Christian and that you want to bless them by giving them the job free of payment."

"Pardon, God?" I exclaimed. "Did you say, *give them the job?* What about my bills and food for the family?"

He simply answered, "Trust Me."

I decided to talk with Kim about this as she is eminently sensible and, to my amazement, she said, "That sounds like God to me!"

We sat down together and wrote the letter, and posted it that same day. Both my business adviser and my solicitor thought I was mad but, because they were Christians, just gave us those knowing looks which said, "Don't come to us when it all goes wrong."

A couple of weeks went by and the day was fast approaching when I would need to settle our accounts with the merchants we had purchased the materials from. We still had no funds to meet our obligation, when we received a phone call from the couple in question asking me to go over as soon as possible to talk with them.

When I arrived at their house they invited me in, sat me down and proceeded to explain that they had never intended to pay my bill. They had chosen my company because I was a small business and had a good reputation. They knew as such I probably would not be able to afford to take them to court and if I did they would only be asked to pay me a small sum each month which I would probably find too troublesome to collect. Yet having received our letter, neither of them had been able to sleep at night because of what they had done and

---

[28] Philippians 4:19 (NASB)

consequently they had arranged with their building society to borrow the necessary funds to pay us. They duly presented me with an envelope which contained the full payment in cash.

We could have chosen to follow the advice we had been given and this was, in fact, what the couple were expecting us to do. We chose rather to act as God had instructed and to trust Him. He ensured that all our needs were met and that we were paid in full. It's God's wisdom we need, not natural wisdom, and at times that might seem foolishness to people around.[29] God's wisdom will always lead us to prosper because that's His plan for our lives. He declares, "I know the plans I have for you ... plans to prosper you and not to harm you, plans to give you hope and a future."[30]

The house move had had a somewhat negative effect on my business. In the days before mobile phones, changing phone numbers three times in three months is never a good thing when you are in a service industry! Work had begun on the conversion of the cinema into the new church building. I felt a strong desire to be involved in the project but all the work had been contracted out and the church had no control over who was awarded the subcontracts. It seemed unlikely that my small company would even be considered for any work but I decided I would go over to Aldershot and speak with the main contractors to see if there was anything I could do. I didn't mind what the work entailed, I would be quite happy with labouring work. I was politely informed that there was nothing for me to do as all the contracts had been awarded months before. I left my card and returned home a little disappointed.

The very next day I was called back to the site by the main contractor and asked if I could do a small job which amounted to a half day's work. It involved working with the Water Board to reconnect the mains supply. I was delighted to take this on as anything was better than nothing. However, when the Water Board official saw the existing pipework, he refused permission to allow their supply to be connected to it. I was promptly awarded the contract to renew all the mains water supply throughout the building – several weeks' work – and once again we were left praising God for His leading and His provision.

---

[29] See 1 Corinthians 1:25
[30] Jeremiah 29:11

The King's Centre duly opened in 1984 and we enjoyed meeting with the church family there. Worshipping with all the congregations in one place was all and more than we dreamt it would be. However, very quickly we had a sense that this was not our home at this moment in time, a feeling that refused to go away. Considering our commitment to the vision, this seemed rather strange and left us somewhat confused!

During this time our business prospered again and life was good. We were enjoying everything we were involved in and felt a great sense of God's blessing on our lives yet knew something was about to happen.

CHAPTER NINE

Our First Church Plant

WE HAD BEEN WORKING WITH Mike Pusey and Peter Gaut in Farnham and the group there began to draw people to their meetings from Bordon, a town some eight miles farther away. We were asked to consider moving again to care for this small group of people, five of them in total. My initial thought was that I did not want to move again, especially to Bordon as I had worked there during my time with British Gas and did not like the area. I had also been asked by another group to consider emigrating to Australia to work with a church there. We had just returned from a holiday in Scotland where we had seen our dream home on the banks of a loch where I was offered a plumbing job. So there seemed to be a lot of choices before us and some decisions to be made!

Bordon is a town in East Hampshire and has a mixed population which includes the armed forces and travellers. We responded to our leaders' request by initially traveling to meet with the small group there and were pleasantly surprised to feel our hearts warming towards them and the town where they were based. Our prayers confirmed that this was indeed the place where God wanted us to be. So goodbye to Scotland and all points in sunnier climes!

Once again our house was on the market and we were moving. During the time it took us to move we met regularly with the group in the home of Dee Phillips, one of the five, and our numbers started to grow as people were getting saved almost on a weekly basis. We eventually moved into our new home in the January of 1987. Moving day was followed by several days of snow which delighted our young children, though not Kim and I so much!

After the first meeting we held in our new home, one of the new believers, Terry, returned knocking on the door and invited me to come outside to see something he had observed on leaving. I went out with him and he took me to the end of my drive and pointed to the sky above our house. Directly above the house was a perfectly circular aura of light like the halo you might see above a saint's head in a medieval painting. There it was hovering over the building. Terry was somewhat taken aback by my reaction as I jumped up and down and danced around the garden, and called the remaining members of the home group to join us out in the garden to see the phenomenon. Afterwards Terry confided to me that he very nearly hadn't come back in because he thought this sort of thing probably happened all the time at Christian meetings and we would think him silly for even commenting on it! For me this sign was God confirming that we had done the right thing in moving. Little did we know what God had in store for us and how much more we were about to be blessed because of this simple step of obedience in moving towns.

Over the next few months I met with a number of Christians and ministers from the town, most of whom commented on what a difficult place it was. This they put down to the amount of satanic activity going on in the area and the ancient ley lines that converged in the town – and who knows what else! Everyone told me that we had little chance of planting a new church in the town. God had laid on my heart the scriptures, "...greater is He who is in [us] than he who is in the world,"[31] and, "If God is for us, who can be against us?"[32] and so I confidently told them that none of that was going to stop us planting a new work there.

Sadly, I have come across this attitude in many Christians and leaders all over the world since. I believe this is due to the fact that they have accepted one of the most common lies that the devil uses – the lie that the place where you are working is one of the most difficult places to be. You see, the devil is the father of lies;[33] his

[31] 1 John 4:4b (NASB)
[32] Romans 8:31b
[33] See John 8:44

battleground is in our minds.[34] If we accept his propaganda and believe his lies to be the truth, we will lose the battle before we even start the fight – a fight which is heavily weighted in our favour as Jesus disarmed our enemy[35] and has placed him under our feet.[36] Father has armed us with the sword of the Spirit which is His Word.[37] If we take Jesus' example found in Matthew 4, where He is tempted in the wilderness, and use that sword skilfully, we will be the overcomers that we are meant to be in every situation. Needless to say our group soon outgrew our lounge and we had to move into a local hall. Most of the growth came through new people getting saved and one spiritualist circle closed down because nearly every member came to faith in Christ.

In those early days, demonic manifestations were commonplace. Our people were mostly fearless and compassionate, and as we commanded the demons to leave, alcoholics got set free, the abused knew freedom and the sick were healed. Brenda, a very well-spoken lady who came to our church from Alton, told me how everyday she would take a hot meal to an alcoholic named Pat who lived in a squat near to her and everyday he would throw the meal at her as she left. She had decided that perhaps she should provide the meals on a plastic plate rather than her best china as she was fast running out!

One day he asked her why she continued to come. She told him that it was because God had told her to show him that God loved him. Within a few weeks Pat asked to come to church and she duly brought him along to our midweek meeting. The fun was only just beginning!

Firstly, Pat refused to get out of the car and appeared to be terrified of coming into the meeting. By the time I was asked to go out to talk to him, he was very upset and swearing and shouting abuse at anyone who came near him in the car; it was clear that he was manifesting something demonic. I asked him to get out of the car, at which point he leapt from the vehicle and started to move around on all fours mimicking the actions of a big cat as he prowled up to me. He roared and spoke in an eerie voice and declared that he

---

[34] See 2 Corinthians 10:5
[35] See Colossians 2:15
[36] See Romans 16:20
[37] See Ephesians 6:17

was going to eat me! I turned to speak to Paul and Peter who had come with me to deal with the situation. I wanted to reassure my friends that all would be well as I had noticed that they were now standing some distance away and were backing off rapidly.

I turned to Pat and commanded him to be free in Jesus' name and for the spirits to come out of him. As I did so, an invisible force lifted him up and threw him across the car park and he landed some feet from me. As we continued to pray for him, he became peaceful and came into his right mind. Within a couple of weeks Pat gave his life to Christ and was set free from his alcoholism and became a very active part of the church as well as finding employment. This sort of thing became almost commonplace in the life of the church.

During the early hours of one morning I was woken by our phone ringing. The call was from the wife of a couple I had recently met who attended a church in a nearby town. I had begun to build a friendship with them. We hosted Ray McCauley from Rhema Ministries in South Africa at our church for a special service and I had invited this couple to join us. On their return home the husband had started acting rather strangely and by the time his wife rang me he was out of control and she was requesting that I went round to pray with him. The situation seemed urgent so I dressed quickly and drove to their house.

I was greeted by the man's mother-in-law and ushered upstairs to the bedroom where she, her husband and daughter were trying to keep the guy under control. It was clear to me that he was demonised and was fully manifesting. His wife and father-in-law were sat on top of him and it was all they could do to keep him on the floor as he was very disturbed. A few weeks prior to this I had listened to some teaching that had encouraged us to minister in a different spirit to the spirit of this world. So in this situation where this man was being very violent I took that to mean that I should minister from a position of peace and nonaggression.

I instructed the wife and father-in-law to get off the man and let him go. As they complied, I realised that the man was holding a twelve-inch carving knife and was completely naked. As soon as he was released he jumped to his feet, made a beeline for me and in an eerie voice told me that he had been waiting for me and was going to kill me and then his children. The knife in his hand was now raised above my head and started to plunge down towards my chest at speed. At just about four inches from my chest the blade seemed to hit an invisible wall in front of me and came to an abrupt stop. As hard as the man tried to push it through and into my chest, he could not and his hand and body started to shake with his efforts. He was a large man and was exerting considerable pressure on the weapon but to no avail. Suddenly it was as if someone had picked him up and I watched as his feet whisked passed my face and he flew across the room and landed in the corner about eight feet away. During his flight he had dropped the knife and we all moved in, laid hands on him gently and started to command the demons who had taken control of him to leave. As we did so, he spat at us and spoke using the foulest of language and making horrible suggestions; his saliva was dripping from the ceiling where he had spat with such force at us and missed.

Some considerable time later peace entered him as all the demons had finally submitted to our commands to leave him. We prayed with him at this point, and he invited Jesus into his life and asked that He would come and fill him with His Holy Spirit, which He graciously did. At this I left them in a relatively peaceful atmosphere to return home, promising to return the next day to talk things through with the family.

The following morning, I discussed with the man about what he had done in order to become so demonised. Proverbs 26:2 tells us that "like a sparrow in its flitting, like a swallow in its flying, so a curse without cause does not alight". I do not believe that people can become demonised without something they have done or an incident in their lives opening the door of their life to these dark forces. It is important to make sure that they are aware of what the open door was and to close it through repentance, and for them to ask God to come and fill them with His Spirit so their house is not left empty for the evil spirits to return with even more, making their latter state worse than their former state.[38] I am pleased to say that having closed that door, he went from strength to strength. He became a good friend, a worship leader in the local church and also an elder there.

---

[38] See Matthew 12:43-45

He is a trophy of God's grace and mercy and looking at him now I find it difficult to believe what we went through with him that night.

The number of drug addicts and alcoholics we were in contact with seemed at times overwhelming and many just wanted to be kept bouncing along the bottom rather than hitting a place where they realised they were the cause of their problems and that they needed to stop blaming everyone and everything else and take responsibility for their own actions. I know that this appears to be an uncaring attitude as every one of them had terrible life stories to tell; but ultimately their bad decisions to deaden their pain through drugs or alcohol only made things worse. I remember being given some wise council that the prodigal son might never have come to his senses and returned home if he had lived in this day and age. He might never have reached rock bottom, eating pig's food, because there are just too many 'do-gooders', people with fine intentions offering a little help but not dealing with the real problem.

Robby was such an alcoholic. He had been bouncing along the bottom for a long while when we came into contact with him. He told us that he wanted to be free and just needed a little support so we invited him to come to stay in our home. We only made one condition: that he didn't drink. Robby managed for a couple of days until one evening he fell out of a taxi that had brought him to our house and wobbled down our drive. I met him at the door. He reeked of alcohol so I would not let him in, much to his displeasure. It had begun to snow and he repeatedly assured me that he had not been drinking despite the evidence of my eyes! It went against all my natural instincts but with two young children in the house, we could not let him stay while he was in such a drunken state. Robby reluctantly staggered away and I later heard that he slept in a ditch until someone else took him in for a few days. Again he caused problems and was back on the street. Eventually he managed to rent a static caravan on a park just down the road from us and turned up at our door, apologized for his behaviour and asked for our help once more. This we gave freely and he seemed to be doing well until one afternoon I returned home to have Kim tell me that the police had been on the phone wanting me to come down to the caravan park. Robby was holed up in his caravan threatening to shoot anyone who came near and demanding to speak to me.

By the time I arrived, there were many police officers surrounding the caravan and the situation was fast deteriorating. It was agreed that I should go and talk with him as I assured the police that to my knowledge he did not possess a firearm. When I entered the caravan, Robby was visibly terrified and it became clear from talking with him that he had upset some of the wrong families in the town and was frightened of retribution being exacted. With his paranoid delusions fuelled by six bottles of vodka, we had come to this place where his home was now surrounded by policemen demanding he surrender himself. After fifteen or twenty minutes I persuaded Robby to give himself up and we both walked gingerly from the caravan to be met by policemen who wanted to frisk both of us, to my surprise, making sure that neither of us had a gun secreted about our persons. Robby was taken away to spend a few nights in a cell, probably the only place he would have felt safe at that time, and I was thanked and let go.

When Robby seemed to be drink-free, I managed to get him a place in a rehab centre in the West Country. Such places were few and far between and they would only take him if he was sober. He assured me that he had not had a drink in a week and would pass the breathalyser test when we arrived. We drove the four-hour journey all the while talking excitedly about the wonderful opportunity he had to once and for all get clean. When sober, Robby was a really pleasant guy. You cannot begin to imagine my disappointment when having arrived at the rehab, they breathalysed him and he failed the test miserably. He had only drunk one bottle of vodka that morning and was more than able to function somewhere near normal on that. The drive back was somewhat quieter and subdued! Try as we did, you simply cannot stop someone drinking if they do not want to – they have to hit rock bottom. There were many more disappointments with Robby as we sought to show him the love of God and eventually we lost contact with him. News came some time later that he had drunk himself into an early grave. I learned so much from encounters like these, about how we should show God's love to the people of this world. Sometimes it needs to be tough love if they are ever to experience the life that God intended for them. The good news is that we saw many people set free from their addictions to go on and live the abundant lives God intended them to have.

CHAPTER TEN

Healings and Warnings

THANKFULLY, WE SAW GOD HEAL and set free so many that people started to travel from towns up to twenty miles away to come to the special healing meetings. During one such evening I spoke on the blind man that Jesus healed (John 9:6). I had heard another preacher speak on this story complete with sound effects. He had asked, "What was the last thing the blind man heard?"

I don't know how you describe that noise that you make deep in your throat as you prepare the ammo to spit in someone's eye but I knew I could do it justice and so I preached the Word with my best sound effects!

When I had finished, we called the sick forward for prayer as was our custom and a lady came forward who was suffering from tunnel vision. She described how it was as if she was looking through pinholes and how this condition was blighting her life. As I started to pray for her, I heard a quiet voice somewhere deep in my spirit say, "You preached it; now is the time to do it. Spit in her eyes!"

A hundred thoughts went through my mind ranging from "Did I clean my teeth this evening?" to "Does my breath smell?" to seriously questioning whether I could actually manage to hit her squarely in the eyes. I imagined saliva running down her face where I had missed the mark. I wondered just how many attempts I would have to make before hitting the target.

The fear grew in me to the place where I just laid my hands on her head and prayed for her without spitting and sent her back to her seat with some kind words. As I was closing the meeting, I noticed her still squinting as she tried to focus. The quiet voice returned deep in my spirit saying, "She isn't healed because you did not do what I told you to do and she could be like that for the rest of her life because of your disobedience."

I was overwhelmed with shame and guilt and knew that I could not send her home without carrying out what God had told me to do. I went to the lady and asked her if she was healed, to which she gave me the response that I already knew in my heart. I gently told her that I had not done what God had instructed me to do.

She replied, "Well, just do what He said!"

I insisted that she knew exactly what this entailed to which she said, "Well, if that's what He said, you had better do it!"

Not trusting my aim, I spat on my thumbs and rubbed them in her eyes. Nothing appeared to happen.

We prayed again and I closed the meeting, and the lady left with everyone else. As Kim and I were leaving, the caretaker called us to look in the ladies' restroom, where one of the cubicles had been vandalised. I imagined the woman being so upset that she went into the toilets and kicked a hole in the door before she left. I have a vivid imagination but felt sure that she must be feeling at the very least humiliated by having someone rub their saliva in her face. After assuring the caretaker that the church would pay for the damage we left feeling sad and disappointed. We really didn't understand why God would ask me to do such a strange thing with no end result.

That night I didn't sleep at all well with so many unanswered questions going back and forth through my mind. Early the next morning the loud ringing of the phone drew me back to consciousness. Half asleep I answered it, to hear a hysterical woman shouting down the phone at me. Having calmed her down, I realised that it was the lady from the evening before. My first thought was that she had phoned to tell me that she was going to sue me for spitting in her eyes! Thankfully, her motive for phoning was the polar opposite. She excitedly informed me that she had just woken up and could see perfectly. Praise God!

I learnt an important lesson that day: never give up on God's Word because His Word never returns to Him without achieving all that He intends it to.[39]

It was about this time that God began to challenge me about my older brother Derek and told me that I should speak to him about his relationship with our father and his relationship with God. He lived in a town nearby but we were never close so we didn't see too much of each other. Derek had become a Christian in his early teens but had turned his back on God sometime later.

There had been a disagreement between him and our dad, and now they did not have anything to do with each other, a situation which caused our parents great pain. I was not sure what I could say to improve the situation. I did, however, have a sense that time was growing short and something needed to be done. Dad was not getting any younger and I did not want my brother to be left with any regrets if Dad should die before they were able to restore their relationship. I decided to drop in and talk to him about the situation.

It was not an easy conversation as we talked about Mum and Dad and his relationship with them and then moved on to his relationship with God. In the end Derek told me that he was not ready to let go of the things that had caused the breakdown between him and Dad; and as for God, maybe one day he would sort that one out as well but he was not ready for that either.

I left his house wondering just why God would send me to my brother when his heart seemed to be so hard. Then, only a few weeks later, I received a call to say that Derek had suffered a "funny turn" and was in the local hospital. I went over to see him and was shocked by what I saw. Although we sat and chatted and the medical staff did not seem to be particularly worried about him, I could see that he was not well and sensed in my spirit that he was not long for this world.

Later that weekend Derek fell victim to a massive brain stem stroke and died.

I had known that he needed to put things right. I knew time was short but did not realise it was *so* short for him. Afterwards, I never knew if my words caused him to have a change of mind about his

---

[39] See Isaiah 55:11

relationship with God, but I do know that he never restored his relationship with our parents, something that would cause them pain for the rest of their lives. There was birthed in me that day a greater urgency to see the people of this world saved, many of whom think they will sort out their relationship with God at some point later but none of us can know just how much time we may have left on this earth.

God, out of His great love and in His grace and mercy, had sent me to give my brother another chance at what he knew to be right. Derek had put off that chance unaware of the urgency. God is sending each one of us to the people of this world with the same offer of forgiveness and eternal life. We need to realise the urgency of the task we have been given and seek to fulfil the Great Commission with greater fervour. People are dying while we allow our fears and apprehensions to stop us.

CHAPTER ELEVEN

Missions Vision is Birthed

THE KING'S CHURCH BORDON was duly launched as we reached forty adults, and continued to grow as we started meeting on a Sunday morning in a newly built community centre which could have been custom built for us. We met in two or three home groups midweek. We soon became the largest church in the town although that was not a difficult thing as most of the others were not of a great size. We had overcome all the negative confessions over the town and planted a new church, proving our God to be greater than any spirit in this world, and around eighty percent of our congregation were new believers.

About this time, I listened to a tape on which the speaker told a story about George Whitefield, who had lived in the 18th century. Whitefield was an English Anglican preacher who also worked in the American Colonies. He preached a series of revivals that came to be known as the 'Great Awakening'. When he walked down the street the presence of God was so powerful that people would come out of their houses, kneel on the pavement and pray, asking God to take control of their lives. I was inspired by this! I imagined and began to believe God for it to happen when I walked down the street. The trouble was, I never walked very far so the likelihood of it happening was very limited and as the thought came to me that "faith without works is dead",[40] I decided that I would make every effort to walk rather than drive whenever possible. My aim was to give God every opportunity to work through my life in the same way!

One Sunday morning, having just arrived in the Community Centre, I busied myself at the front of the hall preparing for the meeting. Then I became aware of a commotion taking place at the door at the back of the hall.

Suddenly a voice rang out loud and clear: "It's all *his* fault!" and I turned to see a woman standing at the entrance pointing directly at me.

I was not sure what, exactly, was 'all my fault' but walked to the back of the hall to talk to the lady. She had arrived at church for the first time and had been welcomed by one of our stewards who had enquired how she had come to find us. It was at this point that she had pointed at me and made her loud declaration.

I was more than a little puzzled as I was convinced that I had never seen her before in my life and was wondering how it could possibly be my doing that she was now standing at the door of our church meeting. On further enquiry she explained that I had walked past her house on a number of occasions in recent weeks and that she had been struck by the thought that I had looked so much like an angel that this particular morning she had decided that she just had to follow me to see where I was going, and that's how she had ended up in our church meeting! We welcomed her in and she stayed for our service.

During the meeting I had a word of knowledge about a woman who was living with a man who was not her husband. Looking around the hall with my natural eyes, I couldn't see anyone whom this might fit. Our visiting lady was no longer in view and I had assumed that she had left the meeting. Moments later one of our ladies Karen came forward and said she felt there was someone in the meeting who was having some physical problems. She shared this word and the visiting lady responded. As she came forward, God told me, "This is the lady who is living with a man who is not her husband."

---

[40] See James 2:26

We prayed for her physical problem and she was healed. At this point I asked her if she was living with someone. She was shocked by the fact that I knew this and within a few minutes had invited Jesus into her life. Some weeks later her partner responded to the change in her life and he too became a believer and without a word from anyone moved out of the house as he felt uncomfortable with their living arrangements. Some eighteen months later I had the joy of seeing them married.

A number of people rather cheekily asked me at the time if her physical problem had been deteriorating eyesight as she had seen me as an angel! I knew a wonderful miracle had taken place that day. God allowed her to see me in the Spirit, as it were, and she just had to follow Him. It has never happened again to my knowledge but I learnt a wonderful lesson that day about the power of a testimony to reproduce itself in the lives of those who hear it in faith and then activate their faith towards God to do the same in and through their lives.[41] I had been challenged by the account of Whitefield and sought to make it my own in some tangible way.

In those early days of the church I learnt to preach by taking Derek Brown's notes, studying them and allowing the truth to settle deep in my spirit, and then a week or two later passing on the teaching to the Bordon people. I felt that this fitted the biblical model where Paul said to Timothy, "The things which you have heard from me ... entrust these to faithful men."[42]

During this time Derek asked me to travel with him to East Germany. When I asked what he wanted me to do he said we would preach the series we had preached recently in our churches. It was one of his series and now I was going to be taking half the sessions for a group of East German believers, with him sitting in the room listening on. The pressure I felt was great but I also felt it was an honour to be trusted to join him. We had a great time, and while we were there the wall between east and west came down and we experienced first-hand an amazing point in history in 1989.

Back home our church was gaining a reputation as a healing church; people came from ever greater distances to receive ministry and the healings continued. We still had hard times when the enemy

---

[41] See Revelation 19:10
[42] 2 Timothy 2:2 (NASB)

sought to challenge our beliefs and, sadly, we buried three dear friends prematurely. Yet each time, in the midst of our grieving, the very next Sunday morning in church I would restate our position that we believe in a healing God and that by Jesus' stripes we are healed[43] and no matter what had happened we still held firm.

It is important to speak out what you believe. Jesus said that if you have faith and believe, whatever you say will happen.[44] James also taught that our tongues set the course for our lives like the rudder of a great ship setting its course.[45] So often we can talk *about* the mountains in our lives rather than speaking *to* the mountains. When you talk about a mountain it only appears to get bigger. When you speak to the mountain in faith, it has to disappear.

During these formative years we were greatly encouraged by visits from Ian Andrews, a man who moves greatly in God's healing power. Ian, often with his wife Rosemary, would come to minister at our monthly healing meetings and we saw God move wonderfully.[46] I count them among my friends.

As the church continued to grow I started to give it more of my time, first one day a week then two, yet still managing to support my family on the income generated from my business in the remaining days of the week. The days were long and I regularly went directly from my plumbing work to pastoral visits, often not returning home until the early hours of the following morning. It became clear that this situation could not continue as I seemed to be holding down two full time jobs, so the church offered to pay me full time to work for them. This was a great blessing although it meant us taking a considerable drop in income as God had provided extremely well for us through the business.

Even this step of faith was tested because soon after we closed the business and started working for the church the interest rates went up 'through the ceiling'[47] meaning that my new salary, which initially had just covered our outgoings, now fell woefully short. We needed

---

43 See Isaiah 53:5
44 See Luke 17:6
45 See James 3:4
46 Publisher's book recommendation: 'Equipped to Heal' by Ian Andrews; ISBN 978-1-907509-17-9.
47 This was in the late eighties.

to move in faith again for our income in a whole new way. God opened a door for Kim to work one night a week and we were also given gifts at times when it seemed we might not meet our bills. God proved again that He is our source of supply.

About this time, I felt God speaking to me about broadening our vision and encouraging the church to think beyond our town and even our country; there is a world out there that needs to know Jesus. I spoke with my friend, Bill Rice, who arranged short term mission teams to go and help churches abroad. I told him that I wanted to give my church a 'missions vision' and asked if he could arrange for me to lead one of his cheaper missions teams, as I explained that most of my people did not earn a great deal. You can imagine my surprise when the missions brochure came out and I was leading the team to Russia, which was the most expensive trip!

My first reaction was far from godly; I was so annoyed and disappointed that I almost refused to lead the team. But God asked me a question. I have learnt that when God asks questions it's not because He needs to know the answer but rather that He wants us to discover it!

The question was simply, "Are you going to carry on moaning about this or are you going to serve this brother and the churches in Russia that you have been asked to go to?"

The answer was equally simple: "Lord, I will serve."

One lady from my church was able to join the team and, along with three others, we found ourselves linked with another small team from Singapore. We travelled to Maykop in Russia, ministering in churches and schools and anywhere that would open their doors to us. It was in the early days just after the Iron Curtain had come down and we were warmly welcomed wherever we went. It was such a privilege to be there at such an historic time, although at night we were confined to our hotel with armed guards to protect us as it was considered too dangerous for us to venture out after dark. This left us with ample time to fellowship with the Singaporean team and their pastor Eric Dooley, originally from the USA. We got on like we were old friends and we seemed to share much in common.

On my return from Russia there was a fax inviting me to go and speak at the New Life Christian Church conference in Singapore and then to go on into Cambodia where Eric was about to relocate his family to start a new church. I had for many years dreamed of returning to south-east Asia, ever since that first trip to Sri Lanka just after Kim and I had married, but a door had never opened. Now it seemed God was blessing me because I had made the decision to serve rather than moan. That was the first of many trips that I made to serve that inspiring, ever-growing group of churches in many nations in south-east Asia – and to think I could have missed it because of my initial unwillingness to serve!

After one such trip to Singapore I met up with some other church leaders from our network in Sri Lanka. We were to minister at a number of conferences as well as working with a few churches. One night during these meetings a man came forward with a large tumour on his neck which had invaded his brain to the point that he could no longer see or hear. We were told that he was only expected to live for a few more weeks and so we prayed for him.

The following evening the second half of our team were ministering there in the tea plantation. During that day the man's hearing had improved a little and, encouraged by this, they prayed again. The next night we were back and he was now seeing and hearing a little more and there were signs that the lump was getting smaller. We repeated this course of treatment, declaring heath and wholeness in Jesus' name, over the next two evenings and each time there was some improvement. Then it was time for us to return home.

The following year I returned to Sri Lanka to minister and on visiting this same church, a man bounded up to me and thanked me for my prayers the year before. I did not recognise him as the tumour had now disappeared altogether and our brother could once again see and hear perfectly. He had been given a clean bill of health from his doctor. Our tag team prayers had set this man free from the cancer that was seeking to take his life. I was reminded of Matthew 18:19 which says that "if two of you agree on earth about anything you ask, it will be done for you by our Father in heaven". Our prayers of agreement night after night had brought about this man's healing. Praise God!

The power of agreement also was brought to bear while I was still working in business. I was carrying out some major works in a house in Camberley in Surrey. During my first day there I had noticed that one of the children was coughing rather a lot and really did not seem to be at all well. I had noticed that there were also bibles around the house and at the end of the day I asked the lady of the house if she believed what the Bible taught, particularly Matthew 18:19. She told me that she was not sure and went away and read the passage again. On returning she assured me that she believed the scripture and so I suggested that we agree that her son would be well by the time I had finished working there at the end of the week.

The boy had been ill for several months and had been into hospital for tests and yet the doctors had been unable to find out what was causing him to be so unwell. So that day we agreed together that he would recover over the days I was working there. The next morning I arrived early and as soon as my van pulled up on the drive the lady of the house opened the front door and ran down the pathway to meet me. My initial thought was to wonder if there had been a problem overnight with the heating but she excitedly told me that since the moment we had agreed in God, her son had not coughed once and had woken that morning feeling perfectly well.

It transpired that they were not Christians but were interested in what the Bible had to say. Over the next few days this lady followed after me as I worked throughout the house, asking me one question after another about God and faith. By the time I had completed the work she had certainly moved much closer in her journey to faith. You see, godly principles will even work with non-Christians if they will choose to apply them!

CHAPTER TWELVE

Challenging Times

ONE MORNING IN THE EARLY NINETIES I woke with a deep sense in my spirit that my time as the pastor of our church had come to an end. Naturally speaking I desperately did not want it to be God speaking to me because I felt that I was living my dreams. As a church we were seeing people saved and healed and God's Kingdom was expanding. I was greatly enjoying my work in the Bordon area. But as the weeks went by it became increasingly clear that the grace for leading the church had left me. I spoke with our senior leader Derek and shared that he might need to find a new pastor for the church as I felt my time had finished and perhaps I needed to go back into secular employment. He counselled me to stick with it but the thought would not go away, and as the weeks and months went by I knew I no longer had the grace for my current role. Where before it had always been a pleasure, no matter how difficult some situations were, now it was just hard work. I started to hand over more and more of the day-to-day running of the church to one of my leaders, Martin, in preparation for him to take over when I eventually moved on, although he was initially unaware of this.

Finally, in 1994, while a wave of laughter was sweeping through churches throughout the world, I was found crying. It seemed that whatever I did I would break down in tears, and the longer it went on, the more convinced I became that I was suffering a breakdown due to the fact that I had failed to do what I believed God to have clearly said to me. Eventually I once again approached our senior leader, as two years had passed since our initial discussion, and explained that I thought I was having a nervous breakdown. He surprised me by telling me that he had thought so too! However, God had revealed to him that I was sowing in tears and led him to that passage at the end of Psalm 126 where it says that those who sow in tears will return with shouts of joy having reaped a harvest. He felt that this scripture confirmed that God was prompting him to release me from my role as the pastor of the satellite church, for me to return to the central church and take up the role as evangelist for the regional work.

As soon as this was agreed, the tears stopped and assurance came from a much unexpected source. Over the years I had only once had any confirmation that what God had said to me in Brussels some twenty years previously would ever come to pass. At that time, attending a conference at the Royal Albert Hall in London led by Reinhard Bonnke, I was called forward by Reinhard. He told me that God had revealed to him that one day I would become an evangelist. This had only served to frustrate me as nothing I did ever seemed to open any doors for this calling to be released and many people continued to tell me that God had called me into business. So, like Mary, I had decided to keep this word in my heart[48] and wait for God to open the doors that no man could shut.[49]

Now, just weeks before I was to be released as the evangelist for our work, I found myself on a trip to Indonesia with Pastor Eric whom I had met in Russia. We were both attending a conference where a man who claimed to be a prophet was teaching, after which people were queuing for him to prophesy over them. I had never come across prophecy being delivered in this manner before and found myself to be very cynical about the proceedings; I could talk with God anytime so why would I need someone else to tell me what He was saying?

Eric was called away to talk with some old friends and I was left sitting with one of his leaders, William from Singapore; a white face in a congregation of dark-skinned people. Immediately I knew I

[48] See Luke 2:19
[49] See Revelation 3:8

would be targeted by this prophet and shared with William, sitting next to me, that during the next session I would be called forward.

He asked me, "What makes you think that?"

I explained my rationale that as I was white, big and blonde, I stuck out like a cue ball on a snooker table amongst all these darker complexions, at which we both laughed – until halfway through the following session, when the prophet looked out into the hundreds sitting before him, fixed his gaze on me and beckoned me forward.

Cynically, I enquired, "What, me?"

To which he replied, "Yes, you come down here!"

My friend watched in astonishment as I walked forward to the front of the auditorium.

To my amazement the prophet recounted to me how in 1975 God had told me, "You will be an evangelist to the nations." He continued, "And when you return home from this conference you will start the ministry that I have called you to all those years ago. Up until now everything has been training and now you start your ministry!"

I was blown away and found myself repenting of my cynicism as I had never divulged to anyone there what God had said to me back in Brussels. And so a new chapter started in our lives...

We handed leadership of the church over to Martin and started to work with the churches in the network, helping to set up evangelistic projects such as Alpha. Our heart was, as it is now, to train people to effectively reach out into their communities and so we set about drawing on much of the experience we had gained through planting the church in Bordon and the pastoral role we enjoyed there.

Some years previously the network of churches had purchased a second-hand double-decker display bus from Bob Gordon of King's Coaches; it was being used rather infrequently so we set ourselves to developing the bus as a mobile youth outreach centre which went to the street corners where disaffected young people hung out. It proved to be an effective tool and was soon going out most nights of the week. This became a full time commitment and so another member of our team, Paul, took on the responsibility for the day-to-day running of the King's Coach.

To our surprise, things took an unexpected turn at this point. I felt God speaking to me about mass evangelism. This was a topic for which I had little time as I firmly believe that we need to empower every member of the church to effectively reach out into the community on a one-to-one basis. Now God seemed to be challenging me to connect with those people who might never come into contact with a believer during everyday life. Even more surprisingly, I felt that He wanted me to purchase a tent as a means to facilitate this approach. My only experience of tent ministry had been of spending one evening shortly after I was saved in a cold, wet marquee at a meeting which was less memorable than the weather. I knew nothing about tents but the thought would not be dismissed, much though I tried, so I arranged to work with a couple of groups I knew of that were involved in tent ministry. One of these was based in Scotland run by John Parsons and the other was 'Christ is the Answer' in Italy.

Working with these two groups only served to remind me of all those negative memories I had of tent ministry, yet God kept pushing me towards purchasing a tent and embarking on just such a ministry! After some discussion with the other leaders on our team it was agreed that I would put together a proposal and costings for a project to purchase a tent and all the equipment to run events. This proposition was eventually agreed upon and we were ready to move ahead.

I approached Miami Missionary Tents in Oklahoma, USA and chose a white modular tent which could seat up to three hundred and fifty people. Just before the equipment was to be purchased the circumstances changed and I was asked not to purchase but to rearrange the project to rent the equipment instead. I was greatly disappointed and I have to say that my response to this request was not very gracious and I started to moan. However, one Saturday morning I awoke from having had a vivid dream in which God had reminded me that He had not told the church to buy the tent but rather that He had told *me* to buy it and that I should stop moaning and get on with it! When I shared this with Kim she jokingly said, "But you promised me that we would never go camping again!"

We spent that morning in discussion and although we only had a few pounds in our account, nowhere close to the ten thousand pounds needed to go ahead with the purchase, we felt it was clearly God leading us. Firstly, we decided to submit this change of venture to the trustees who had made the request not to buy as we did not want to seem to be rebelling against their decision. To our surprise they offered to lend us the finance for six months to enable us to go ahead and purchase the tent and to look to repay the loan within that timeframe. This enabled us to order the tent and start to plan missions for the upcoming season.

On receiving notification from Tilbury Docks that the tent was ready to be collected, I hired a truck and headed up to the Port of London terminal with no little trepidation as I really did not know what to expect. Fortunately, the tent just fitted into the vehicle but with very little space to spare as the canvas and poles were much bigger than I had envisaged!

A few days later, after my return home, a group of friends met in the grounds of a local Christian conference centre in Whitehill to erect the tent for the very first time. The instruction manual was a little smaller than expected as it consisted of only one page of A4 paper with a few drawings on one side and some notes which made little sense to any of us – except to Kim, who had no experience with erecting tents at all and so was not hampered with thinking, "This is how it should go." It did indeed transpire that our previous experience of handling tents was hindering our understanding of just how this tent worked; something I have often experienced in church circles since on a variety of subjects!

What we 'know', our past experience, can hinder us from doing what God is calling us to do. Moses experienced something similar when the people of God needed water a second time while in the wilderness.[50] Moses had already struck the rock once with his rod and water had come forth and everyone had drunk. Now, in the second instance, God tells him to speak to the rock and water will come forth. But Moses' rationale is, "I've done this before... I know how to do this," and so he strikes the rock. The scary thing is, *water flows* but God pronounces that because Moses has not followed Him wholeheartedly, he will not enter the Promised Land.

We have to be so careful that we don't allow what we think we know to stop us from stepping into all that God has planned for us. God wants us to have a relationship with Him, not just to learn a few

---

[50] See Numbers 20:8

formulae to enable us to achieve some extraordinary goals. Kim's approach to the task of erecting the tent with no preconceptions – a clean sheet – meant she was better prepared to understand how it all came together; a lesson learnt after some six hours of a team of guys battling with the canvas and poles. Then we listened to Kim's interpretation of the instructions and, lo and behold, the tent soon stood before us in all its glory. Fitting it out with wiring for lighting and sound took a few days, then we took it all down again and packed it away, sure that we were ready for our first mission.

On the day of that first mission on Butt's Green in Alton, and despite all our prayers, the weather was possibly the worst it could have been to put up a tent which was twenty-nine feet in diameter on a green in the small market town. The rain was the heaviest we had seen in a few months and conditions were made worse by the wind which was gusting at up to seventy miles per hour. This at times took hold of the canvas which was tethered at several points to the ground and, momentarily lifting the poles and fabric off the ground, turned the tent into the largest wind chime in Hampshire as it dangled a few feet about the turf. Yet before we could pull it down the wind would die and flatten the canvas on the ground again. After spending the whole morning trying to get what seemed like a huge canvas erected I was at the point of giving up and almost in tears.

We were all soaked to the skin and the water was running down my back when some ladies from the church arrived with lunch for us. We were persuaded to stop to eat and assured that the whole enterprise would go better after we had eaten and rested. If anything it was raining harder as we finished our meal and the wind was still blowing hard. One faithful lady, Pam Robertson, convinced us that we should pray before we started again and I remember her prayer to this day; she simply asked God to make the wind work *for* us rather than *against* us as it had been all morning. As we took to our task, a gust of wind again hit the canvas lifting it into the air but no sooner had it done this than the wind died away completely dropping the centre pole exactly where it needed to be, and before the next gust arrived we were able to secure the ropes and there the tent stood before us.

We had struggled all morning but the moment we invited God to get involved He stepped in and all our troubles were overcome! That week the weather was less than wonderful but the tent attracted many people who came in, enjoyed the events and heard the Gospel preached in many different ways and went away with a positive impression of the church. Opportunities were birthed to further develop relationships in the weeks and months ahead.

God was so good to us and within the timeframe that the church had stipulated for us to repay the loan of ten thousand pounds, we had not only cleared the debt but had also purchased a large load lugger trailer which provided storage for the tent as well as a practical means to transport it to the various venues where we were being invited to run events.

Over the next couple of years, the number of 'Tent Events' expanded and we purchased more equipment, which meant we could no longer transport it all in our trailer which had served us well but now was just too small. The advice I received was to invest in a 7.5 tonne truck to haul all our gear, but we had nowhere near enough funds to finance this upgrade.

It was at this point that I received a phone call from a friend, Adrian, who had been approached by a company who were experiencing financial difficulties. He was offered the opportunity to buy a 7.5 tonne truck at a knockdown price as they required funds quickly. Adrian did not need the truck himself but knew its history and had serviced it regularly so knew that it was a bargain at several thousand pounds under the market value. As the asking price almost exactly matched the money we had in our bank account, the deal was done. Once again God provided what we needed when we needed it.

The 'Tent Event' ministry continued to expand and with each event we gained a growing reputation with the churches we were working with across southern England as we helped them to raise their profile within their communities. Many of the churches we worked with were being pressurised by their local authorities to repeat the events in the following years as the events were being so well received by the communities. In addition, churches were being approached to get involved in other community events being run by their local authorities, which was great!

CHAPTER THIRTEEN

Expect Great Things from God

DURING THIS TIME, WE HAD BEEN ASKED to help a church in Kettering who were about to be left without a pastor as their current leaders, Charles and Rachel, had felt called to move on to establish a Christian retreat centre. The church had not seen growth for a number of years and we were happy to take on the challenge to believe to see the situation turn around, and committed ourselves to supporting them for a year.

Kettering is eighty miles north of London and is famous for its boot and shoe industry which, sadly, has declined since the 1970s due to overseas competition.

We felt it right to help, following a word which the Lord had impressed upon us from Luke 13:5. This passage tells of a fig tree in a vineyard that had not borne any fruit in three years. The owner instructed his gardener to cut it down but the gardener protested that he would give the tree special attention for a year to see if any figs appeared and so the tree was reprieved.

We travelled to Kettering two or three times a week. Usually this would take two-and-a-half hours each way but just occasionally that could triple due to adverse traffic or weather conditions on the M1/M25. The people there were lovely and we developed many friendships, and God gave us an amazing grace and strength for the travelling. We also enjoyed support from various friends who helped with the work. The people started to grow in their faith and things seemed to be going well.

During this first year we sought God on a number of occasions as to whether we should move house to the town but always felt that this was not what God had called us to do. At the end of the first year we had still not seen any numerical growth but agreed with the church that they had grown in many other ways as situations came to light and were resolved. We committed ourselves to support the church for a second year during which the congregation started to grow numerically and it looked quite feasible that we would comfortably meet the targets the church had set themselves and possibly exceed them. Again we asked God if we should relocate to Kettering and again we felt Him put a check on such a move. As the second year was coming to an end we felt so much had been achieved regardless of whether they had met their targets and that we should stay for a third year.

Sadly, at this point things started to come apart; unresolved issues came to the surface and people left rather than face them. Towards the end of our second year the church was well short of the target they had set themselves and there was a great deal of disappointment. At this point the elders came to us and said that they felt that we had done our best but it was time to close the church and for everyone to move on. I have to say that it was very difficult for me to accept this. We agreed to continue to meet midweek for a few months as Kim and I helped individuals to find other churches in the area where they felt God might be adding them. It was now apparent to us why God had not allowed us to move to Kettering although He had sent us to help. We have since learnt from working with a number of churches that have found themselves in difficult times that there has to be a desire to change; if not, there can be no lasting fruit, either spiritually or numerically. It is so important to let go of things from the past. Holding onto unresolved issues rather than dealing with them, or persisting with antiquated structures rather than letting the Holy Spirit move you forward, will always cripple the church and prevent her from bearing fruit. Foundations are also important; trying to build on a faulty foundation is like building on shifting sand. Just as something appears to be rising up it can completely collapse with little or no warning. Churches need to be planted on the foundation of Jesus with their purpose being guided by clear, God-given vision and being established on New Testament principles.

Shortly after our time in Kettering came to an end in 2004, God planted a phrase in my spirit: "Expect great things from God and do great things for God." This saying became my daily confession and everywhere I preached I encouraged people to take it on board and to live lives that expect great things from God and are willing to do great things for Him. Over the coming months, the more I reached out for God, the more He moved, and the more I attempted to do for Him, the more success we saw.

One Sunday, having preached in a church in Haslemere and encouraged them to join me with my confession, a man came to me and told me that God had given the same confession to William Carey, the founder of the Baptist Mission Society which was formed in Kettering. I was completely unaware of this! Carey had spent his early life there until leaving as a missionary to India in 1793. He had earned a meagre living making shoes from leather which he purchased from a man in Northampton. The story continues that the man was so disappointed with the finished product that he told Carey that he should stop wasting his leather and that he would support William directly in his ministry instead.

Immediately I felt God say to me that because we had been faithful to His direction over the previous two years, He had placed on us something of the same anointing that He had placed on William Carey for world mission and that Father God would honour our confession just as He had honoured Carey's. Very humbling and exciting! Little did we realise the opportunities that God was going to open up for us worldwide. I learnt again that day that disappointment and failure are only the battle scars of those who are prepared to do great things for their God. They are but the stepping stones into our destinies and unless we are willing to embrace them we run the risk of never seeing beyond the fear of failure and will always be bound by it, totally hamstrung in any attempt to work great ventures for our God.

Over the next year we saw God increasingly bless our work; we launched a healing ministry called the 'Healing Hour' and opened the doors of the church building twice a week for an hour to pray with whomever came through those doors. A team of committed church members staffed this and saw God do some amazing things. Our motto, of course, was, "Expect great things from God and do great things for God," and our regular prayer was from Acts 4:29-30: "...enable your servants to speak your word with great boldness. Stretch out your hand to heal and perform signs and wonders through the name of your holy servant Jesus." This was just what happened as they spoke and prayed boldly; God healed cancers, restored damaged bodies and set free those who were oppressed by the devil. Let me encourage you to make our confession and prayer your regular confession and prayer and see what God will do through you!

On one occasion we prayed with an older gentleman who was suffering from prostate cancer. Each month he received an injection of a drug to slow the progress of the cancer which he had been told would have to be administered for the rest of his life. The medical profession could not cure his cancer, he told us, but could slow its progress so that it would not kill him. After we had prayed together he attended the hospital for his scheduled appointment only to be informed that he could not receive his usual medication. This panicked him as he thought his treatment had become the subject of government health cutbacks! But he was assured that this was not the case and that, rather, it was because his blood test showed a normal blood count and the drug was only given in proportion to the measure of any abnormality. He continued to go for blood tests for some months, never having any need of an injection again, and to all intents and purposes is healed from his condition.

One lady who visited the Healing Hour was complaining of a back problem. She was ministered to and experienced a complete healing. The next morning, she was able to get out of bed without any help from her husband, something she told us that she had been unable to do for some months. She was so shocked by this that she decided to test her healing further and so visited the gym for a workout including some weightlifting. She returned home having confirmed to herself that she was indeed healed. Later she told us that she had been on the waiting list to have a rod inserted up her spine to help support her body, so dire were her back problems.

The following week she brought her six-year-old son along with her. The lad had been excluded from school due to his bad behaviour caused by his ADHD. After we prayed for him he went home and asked to go to bed, a request quite unknown by his parents! Prior to this the boy had managed on very little sleep. He slept the afternoon away and when she and her husband eventually woke him, the boy was soaking wet from perspiration and declared that all the "bad things" had left him. His behaviour change was demonstrated by his ability to play happily with other children and the lad was eventually allowed to return to school.

Many of our team members experienced God working through them in similar ways to these two accounts and saw many people who came through our doors set free from various ailments and diseases.

CHAPTER FOURTEEN

Children of the King of Kings

IN 2004 I WAS TRAVELLING with a team to Sri Lanka preaching in churches and encouraging the believers. In a conversation with Pastor Roshan Wickremasinghe from Columbo he asked what I was involved in back in the UK. I explained what we were doing with the tent to which he replied that he thought that this model would also work well in Sri Lanka. As I was leaving his office, I clearly heard God say to me, "Give him a tent so that he can also reach the communities of his nation."

On my return home I started to seek God for the money to purchase Roshan a tent. But unlike when we initially bought our marquee, the money did not materialize and several months passed without a penny appearing. I knew something was wrong but was not sure exactly what. Every time I talked to God about it, He just repeated what He had originally said to me: "Give Roshan a tent." Finally, I realised He was telling me to give this pastor *my* tent!

Now that was not a message I was ready to hear. I was enjoying being involved in all that we were doing with the tent and it was one of the greatest faith ventures I had ever been through. Now here was God telling me to give it all away. But God persisted as He does and eventually I gave in and agreed that at the end of the summer season we would ship the tent to Sri Lanka as a gift to His work out there.

I was not sure how this was going to be worked out but I was equally sure that God had it all in hand. On the final day of the last mission we were running that year in Haslemere in Surrey, we were just preparing to pack up the tent and all the equipment when a Christian walked onto the site on Lion Green with his friend Rodney who was visiting from Sri Lanka. Rodney told us that he was an evangelist and had come to see the tent. As we talked, I shared how we were planning to send the tent to his home country and it transpired that he knew the pastor we were sending the equipment to, which was a great blessing to him as he had been praying for a tent to use. He also gave me the business card of a friend of his who ran a shipping company that transported all manner of items to Sir Lanka.

After several phone calls, and a few weeks later, I was driving our truck to Tilbury Docks to deliver the tent to the shipping company. I still had no idea what it would cost to ship the marquee but that morning an envelope had arrived in the post with a cheque for two hundred and fifty pounds from someone who had heard of our intentions and had wanted to help towards the costs of exporting the tent. You could not imagine my surprise when, having weighed the tent and poles, the shipping agent announced that the cost would be two hundred and thirty pounds. I was so blessed, and on the way home I asked God why the cheque was for two hundred and fifty pounds when the shipping was less than this figure. The answer became clear as I realised that I had spent twenty pounds on fuel to make the journey to the docks. God is no man's debtor; He had covered everything!

Having waved goodbye to the tent as it set sail for a distant shore, we now found ourselves with somewhat of a dilemma. We had already committed ourselves to running 'Tent Events' in a number of locations. As pastors began to hear via the grapevine that we were no longer in possession of a marquee, some interesting telephone conversations ensued.

My assurances that I was only responding in obedience to God's leading and that I was convinced that Father had everything in hand were met with varying degrees of graciousness. The truth of the matter was that I had no idea at that particular moment in time how exactly God was going to sort out this state of affairs.

As I prayed into the situation, I felt God tell me to buy an even bigger tent. When I asked, "Just how big?" I felt Him say, "As big as you can believe Me for!" I revisited Miami Tent's website and decided to order the 133' x 61' blue and white striped modular marquee with telescopic masts, having learned from our experience on Butt's Green! This tent could seat from three hundred and fifty to fifteen hundred depending on which configuration was erected.

Once again our church offered to underwrite the cost for six months after which we would need to repay them. This time, as I had learnt some lessons about faith, I told God that I wanted to pay for the tent before we even started to use it. Yet again God outstripped our expectations and the day before we went to the docks to pick up the new tent we were in a position to repay the loan and we started our mission's diary debt-free.

Once again we needed a dry run to put the tent up and kit it out for power and lighting and other equipment. A team of guys met in the grounds of Waverley Abbey House, CWR's conference centre in Farnham, as this new tent was just too big for Whitehill Chase. Again the instructions were limited to just one sheet of paper but this time our experience helped us and the tent went up with few problems.

Once the canvas was in place and securely fastened, I walked around inside the empty tent pondering on just how vast this new model seemed. I was joined by a friend who asked me, "What were you thinking, buying a tent this big?" The tent was so large that his words bounced back from the far wall: "What were you thinking... what were you thinking..."

At that point fear and uncertainty came knocking at my door and for a little while I started to wonder if I had indeed gone too far and perhaps we would never use the tent to its full capacity. Yet faith was rekindled a few days later when through the morning post I received Reinhard Bonnke's newsletter celebrating his ministry in Africa. I opened it and there was a photograph under which the caption read, "Reinhard's first tent seated 35,000 people," and I clearly heard God say to me, "See, you just don't think big enough!" Our new tent in its largest form seated only fifteen hundred people. That's a lesson we all need to learn; our God is able to do far more than we think or can imagine if we will but trust Him.[51]

During the week in which we had the tent up to work on it, I had issued a blanket invitation to everyone in the church to come over

---

[51] See Ephesians 3:20

and view our new resource, but few managed to find the time to do this. To be honest, I was desperately disappointed and to my discredit started to moan once more, which is never a good thing! Early one morning I was driving into my office mulling over my frustration and as I passed a newly built retirement complex, Beaumont Village, God stopped me in my tracks. This project had been undertaken by a member of the congregation and God reminded me that he too had issued an invitation to an open day – an open day to which I had not found the time to attend for one reason or another.

Right there and then, God told me, "See! You reap what you sow!" I turned my car around and drove into the complex's car park, marched into the office and was soon being shown around the facility by Jim. All I could see was how wonderful this complex was and would have loved to have given my parents the opportunity to spend the rest of their days there as they were increasingly finding it difficult to cope in their home. However, the purchase price was way beyond what they, my sister or I could afford, in order to buy a flat. So I left moaning in much the same way as I had arrived!

As I drove out through the gates, God posed me a question: "Are you a son or a slave?" I stopped the car and thought for a moment, and answered at the top of my voice, "I am a son of the living God," to which He replied, "Then start acting like one. What do you want?"

The answer was quickly on my lips: "One of those flats for my parents, if they would like it."

Father responded just as quickly, "Then go and buy one!"

I reversed my car back into the car park, strode purposefully into the sales office and announced that I would like to buy a flat for my parents. Jim, quite reasonably, asked me a question which I should have seen coming. His question was simply, "Which one?"

Not wanting to seem unprepared, and buoyed up by my newfound understanding of sonship, I declared, "I would like to have the show flat." Having viewed the various abodes available, this was the one that I felt my parents would like best. That afternoon my parents, my sister and I all went to view the flat and, as everyone approved, it was agreed that Mum and Dad would move in right away and we could then sell their current home without a chain hindering the process.

The only problem was that we were twenty-five thousand pounds short of the agreed purchase price and Kim and I were the only ones that knew it, as I didn't see fit to let my parents and Jane know about this small wrinkle. Over the next few weeks our trust in God would be rewarded as first one gift and then another and finally a third came in, the last of which arrived just a few days before we were to complete the transaction.

Kim and I had not told anyone of the shortfall but God knew and provided wonderfully. You see, when we have a proper understanding of who we are in Him – that we are His sons and daughters, joint heirs with Jesus – then nothing is beyond us or impossible for us. Our adopted Father is the Lord, the Creator of the heavens and the earth. He has limitless resources available to us. That morning when God had asked me if I was a son or a slave, for the first time in my Christian experience I grasped the reality of our heritage in Father – that on the day I became a Christian, I became a son of the living God with all the rights and privileges that entails – and the truth of that revelation dropped the eighteen inches from my head to my heart. There is a danger that as believers we can walk around our whole Christian life just like I had, never really understanding the ramifications of the simple truth that we are children of the living God. Yes, we may have an academic understanding of the notion and can probably quote all the supporting scriptures but God wants us to have more than just an intellectual understanding; He wants us to have a daily, vital experience based on the knowledge of His Fatherhood.

Shortly after I experienced this breakthrough I had the opportunity to meet the Princess Royal, HRH Princess Anne, our Queen's daughter. Princess Anne was coming to officially open Beaumont Village where Mum and Dad were now living. As we were waiting for her to arrive, all dressed in our smartest clothes, everyone in the room was very nervous, making frequent visits to the bathroom, no doubt to check makeup and straighten ties, according to gender of course! It was all very exciting.

Then there she was, walking around the room shaking people's hands. I began to wonder if Princess Anne quite realised just whom she was about to meet. I say it with the utmost respect, but she is only the daughter of our Queen and here she was about to meet a son of the King of Kings! Knowing who you are in God changes everything; your perspective is completely different; what might have seemed impossible is suddenly achievable and you no longer need to be concerned about lack of resources as our Father has limitless resources.

We need to realise this fundamental truth. The trouble is that many of us were brought up in families where resources were stretched. I guess I was about twelve years of age when I first realised that there were families that had and families that did not have as much! I was very keen on water sports, especially canoeing. I really wanted to have my own canoe but when I asked my father if he would buy me one he told me that they did not have the money for such items. Dad encouraged me that if I really wanted a canoe of my own then I should get a job and save to buy it myself. I managed to find a job delivering papers which meant every morning I would be up at 6am to ride to the newsagent to pick up my papers and deliver them before setting off for school. This I did come rain or shine, storm or snow, and I received the princely sum of one pound per week. With the cost of the canoe being twenty pounds and a further ten pounds for a paddle and a life vest, I resigned myself to my early morning start for the best part of seven months. Eventually the joyous day arrived when I was able to purchase said canoe.

Down to the water I went and very happily paddled up and down the river. A friend saw me and asked if he could have a go in my canoe which I willingly let him do. On returning to the bank he declared that he wanted one just like mine. I told him that the canoe cost twenty pounds and the paddle and life vest were another ten pounds and that he would probably have to get a job and work for at least thirty weeks to earn enough money to pay for them. The very next week I was there again on the river paddling up and down when I saw someone else launching a canoe from the riverbank slightly ahead of my position. As I paddled over, I realised that it was my friend. When I asked him how he had managed to get his canoe so quickly he told me that his father had bought it for him immediately. In that moment I realised that some fathers were richer than others. When we become Christians we are adopted into God's family and our heavenly Father has limitless resources. It no longer matters whether our earthly fathers are wealthy or not; our heavenly Father "owns the cattle on a thousand hills"[52] and, whatever He asks of us, He is more than able to supply whatever we need to fulfil the task He has called us to do.

It struck me that the Queen never worries about what she will need for any particular duty required of her. Her Royal Majesty has confidence that whatever she needs will be available to her just when she needs it to be. So often worry and fears about the resources we might require can stop us from stepping into all that God has for us to do. We need to realise that everything we need will be provided at the precise moment it is required.

---

[52] Psalm 50:10

CHAPTER FIFTEEN

God Proves Ever Faithful

SHORTLY AFTER MY PARENTS MOVED into the retirement village, my Mum was diagnosed with breast cancer. The doctor informed us that he could get her through an operation to remove the cancer but at her age the main problem would be two to three days after surgery when there was a high risk of heart failure due to the shock to her system. This was a difficult time for us as a family but my parents, who were not believers, bravely decided that Mum should go ahead with the surgery.

Just as the doctor predicted, Mum came through the operation and seemed to be recovering well. Then three days later Kim and I arrived at the hospital ward for visiting hours and were greeted by the rest of my family standing in the corridor with the curtains closed around Mum's bed. There seemed to be a frenzy of activity going on in the bay. Our hearts sank and we all stood around waiting anxiously to hear what was happening. It seemed that, sadly, the doctor's expectation was correct and Mum had suffered a heart attack; the medical staff were seeking to resuscitate her as we were standing outside. I prayed and reminded God that I had trusted my parents' salvation into His hands.

Early in my Christian life, filled with zeal, I had desperately tried to encourage my parents to become Christians but both had strongly told me that religion was not for them and it was only a phase that I was going through. The more I pushed, the stronger their responses were until one day they banned me from ever speaking about my faith to them ever again. This devastated me as I realized that I had blown it with them and I also knew the Scriptures taught that I should honour my parents and respect their wishes, but I certainly didn't relish being unable to raise the subject of my faith again.

Over the years I was encouraged as God brought Christians across their path at times of need, and booklets and tracts they had been given were passed on to me with a short explanation of how they had come by them. But nothing seemed to change the way they felt about Christianity, and it was clear to me that something buried deep in their past had closed the door to God and they were keen on keeping it closed.

Now faced with Mum's imminent death, here I was reminding God that I was trusting Him for my parents' eternal future. God did not need prompting, though, as He was already at work in a most amazing way. After about half an hour a doctor came out to us and explained that Mum's heart had stopped but they had managed to resuscitate her, and that she would need to be moved to an intensive care bed. She was still not 'out of the woods' but, praise God, she was alive and over the next few weeks did eventually make a full recovery.

As we were chatting shortly after her return home, Mum shared with me what had happened that day at the hospital from her perspective. She told me that she was lying in bed looking at the photo of her great-grandson George on the bedside cabinet when she felt someone grab her from behind by the neck of her nightgown and drag her from the bed. She initially thought it was the man in the bed beside her, who was a little disturbed, but instead of falling to the floor she was pulled through the ceiling. She could still see her bed and the photo of her great-grandson beside it in the distance but it was moving farther and farther away.

Mum told me how she could feel a great white light behind her which was beginning to burn her skin. She recounted how instantly she knew that she was being taken before God to be judged for her life and instinctively knew that she was not ready. She went on, "I got down on my hands and knees and started to drag myself back to the bed where I could still see the photo of George, and eventually I managed it and opened my eyes to see the doctor standing over me, having restarted my heart with the paddles." At this point she looked at me and asked, "What do you think this means?"

When I replied, "I think you know, Mum!" she smiled a smile of recognition. God had given her a first-hand experience of death and what is to come for those who are not ready. I am sure over the next few weeks she made her peace with God and when she eventually died sometime later I am sure that she was ready. At her funeral I was able to remind everyone of her experience, as she had told anyone who would listen what had happened to her during that fateful stay in hospital.

Dad never really recovered from Mum's death, as they had shared so much together and since he had lost his hearing she had been his ears to the world. Now he was faced with his worst fear: life without the one person who had been his strength through all the hard times. Living in the village proved to be a blessing as people gathered around him and he started to experience the love of God through the Christians that ran the village and others that came in. This love was eventually to break through when one day Helen, one of the Christians there, prayed with Dad as he asked God to be part of his life. He never told me this personally but that was not unusual as he was a somewhat reserved person and had been brought up to believe religion and politics were private matters and not to be discussed. The fact that he would pray openly with someone was truly amazing. So God once again proved faithful even with a couple whom life had hurt and caused to close themselves to Him. He won through.

The last time I saw Dad we had spent a great day together. As I was leaving on a trip to Sri Lanka the following day, I had dropped in to remind him I would be away for a few weeks. As I left the village I felt God say, "That's the last time you will see your dad." I was not sure what that meant as Dad seemed in good health and the political situation in Sri Lanka at the time was very volatile with the civil war raging once more. There had been a number of times in the past when we had found ourselves in dangerous situations on the island and I did not want to assume that I would not be faced again with a threatening scenario. Having taken my leave of Dad, I returned home and made sure our life insurance was up to date and that Kim was aware of how to access our bank account just in case it was I who was not returning from the trip abroad!

So I boarded the plane and flew to Sri Lanka to fulfil what God had asked me to do there. Towards the end of the trip I got a call from Kim to say that Dad had suddenly been taken ill and was now in hospital. As soon as she broke the news I knew what God had said to me would be true; I would not see my father again. I explained to Kim what He had said to me. Friends in Sri Lanka arranged for me to return home a couple of days early as it was apparent my family needed me to be with them, but even before I departed from Colombo Airport, Dad had passed away and was reunited with Mum in glory. God was so good to me as I had enjoyed such a good time with Dad that last day together. He prepared me for the shock of losing my father while so far away from home and family. I am so grateful to God for all that He did with my parents in bringing them to Him and restoring our relationship. I am also grateful to my parents for all they sowed into me and the lessons they taught me which have enabled me to stand firm in my faith.

CHAPTER SIXTEEN

The Year of the Open Door

BUYING THE BIGGER TENT had again put pressure on our transport provision and if we were to be involved in bigger events we needed a second vehicle. We had managed for a year with a little transit van in addition to our truck but soon realised we needed a second 7.5 tonne lorry. I started to pray that God would provide us with a second vehicle and within a couple of days returned home to find one parked in the hammerhead outside our house. I was amazed how quickly God had answered and fully expected to find the keys with a note pushed through our letterbox, and so was extremely puzzled when they were not there on the doormat. Yet the truck did not move. It stayed parked outside our house, which was a little unusual as we live at the end of a residential cul-de-sac.

Each day I claimed the truck as God's provision and told Kim to expect to see the keys come through the door. Days and weeks went by and the vehicle did not move, and the neighbours started enquiring after the ownership of the lorry. I kept true to my confession that it was mine as God had brought it to my door.

One morning as I was leaving for the office, I noticed a young man from a family in the next street trying to start the truck. Chatting with him, I discovered that he had bought the truck to start a business but had now changed his mind and just wanted to sell it quickly as he could not pass the relevant driving test. He had been offered a few thousand pounds and had decided to accept it although it was well below the market value. Here he was, trying to start the truck up to take it to the dealer. So I asked if he would accept four thousand pounds from me instead and he could leave it where it was, a proposition to which he agreed with some sense of relief.

I phoned Derek and recounted the morning's events and he offered to lend me a thousand pounds to add to the money sitting in our account, and so the deal was struck. A jumpstart from my car caused the lorry to immediately burst into life and I climbed in and drove it to the farm where we store all our equipment. That day we had secured our second vehicle and were set up to do bigger events!

I guess you know what I am about to tell you... Within a month we had been given a number of gifts and the loan was repaid and the money was back in our account. Isn't our God good? Both of our trucks have served us well and made regular trips relatively trouble-free. God has even blessed us through a friend, Adrian, who carries out our annual servicing and MOTs. Praise God, He is so good!

At the beginning of 2004 I was praying about how we might increase what we were doing with the tent ministry as it seemed to me that it was a big investment in terms of the Kingdom and should be used more than our limited summer weather allowed. As I prayed, God told me not to worry as He was about to open a door for us to take the tent into Europe where the weather improved earlier in the year. I had no contacts at all in Europe so knew it would have to be God. For our church, 2004 was prophesied to be the "year of the open door" which dovetailed perfectly with what God was impressing upon me personally and so I was eagerly expectant.

Towards the end of January, I was attending a conference that I had felt I should go to. While there, the only person I met whom I remotely knew was a friend of a friend, and I was the only person there that he recognized, so we linked up and spent our spare time chatting. Eventually we started to talk about the tent ministry and, to my surprise, Charles announced that he thought it would work well with the group of churches his son Craig was involved with in Bulgaria; he asked me if I would be willing to take the tent there. All I knew about Bulgaria was that it was in Europe, and my spirit jumped within me, realising this could be the door that God had told me about. I told Charles about what the Lord had said to me earlier in the month and he agreed to contact his son and make the connection between us.

A few weeks later I received an email from Craig saying that they would really like us to come down and do two missions on the understanding that we preached a full Gospel message and were willing to pray for the sick, believing God for signs and wonders to follow. I, of course, replied that I would *only* be willing to come if they allowed me to preach a full Gospel message and to minister to the sick, believing for signs and wonders to follow!

At this point my lack of geographical knowledge brought me to a shocking discovery. I had committed myself to be in Bulgaria in two months' time with a truckload of equipment and I thought that it might be a good idea to find out exactly where the country is located. I purchased a road map of Europe to start to plan the journey and realised that the town we were going to in Bulgaria was some sixteen hundred miles away and the journey would necessitate us passing through some ten countries, a number of which were outside the European Union. As I sought to get advice on what we would need to make the journey, the main consensus was not to even try to do it! I was filled with horror stories of how it could take weeks to get there if we ever managed to reach our destination at all. Tales of nightmarish proportions regarding days spent queuing at border crossings were common and various Christian organisations who heard of our plans kindly phoned me to tell me of their negative experiences while trying to make similar journeys. They told me how they had been turned back from borders for not having paperwork that they had no idea was required or was impossible to obtain from back home in England.

But in all this I felt sure that God had opened the door for us to go and would open the borders as well. Our friend Jools offered to help by finding out all that we needed to make the trip and spent many hours researching and contacting trucking agencies, embassies and exploring the Internet looking for information that would help us to go through the door that God had opened for us. Still the negative comments flowed and eventually, just two weeks before we were due to set off, the couple who had offered to help with the driving dropped out, saying that they thought it was unlikely we would make it. This was a tremendous blow and I wondered how I could make the trip on my own as it seemed impossible to find replacement drivers at such short notice. It had been much more difficult than I had imagined in the first place as I had rather naively thought that people would be queuing up to volunteer to take part in this adventure, but it transpired that the spirit of adventure was now somewhat lacking in the church for my particular venture!

I decided that if I was to do it on my own then I would need to leave as soon as possible. There was, however, one problem in that I was booked into our church's national leaders' conference and felt I needed to make my apologies for dropping out at the last minute. I arranged to see Derek and explained the situation. His first question was, "Are you sure it's God's will to go?"

I explained what God had said to me at the beginning of the year and how the only door that had opened was this one so I felt sure it was right. Derek agreed and promised to find me two replacement drivers at the conference the following week. Praise God, two drivers volunteered and we were back on track!

The truck was loaded and we set off for Dover, and everything was going well although we did make a couple of wrong turns in Germany which cost us some time and added over a hundred miles to an already long journey. As we entered Eastern Europe we realised many of the horror stories we had been told were based in truth; border crossings were difficult, with almost every official looking for a bribe which we firmly refused to pay with a smile and "I don't understand" and after a short delay we were let through.

While traveling through Serbia we discovered that there was a fuel shortage and that diesel for our truck was being rationed. We were constantly on the lookout for petrol stations with stocks of fuel to enable us to keep the truck moving. This was just about possible in the larger towns but once we ventured further afield, petrol station after petrol station was closed. On one occasion we travelled for nearly an hour with our fuel gauge registering on empty and I knew that we must be running on fumes! We had no choice but to press on, praying that we would find a garage which was open and had fuel. As we were praying, a fuel tanker pulled out onto the road in front of us. We didn't know if it was full or was empty but felt God telling us to follow it. This we did for a number of miles until eventually it pulled into a petrol station and we watched as the driver prepared to fill the tanks. Seeing us watching, he enquired if we needed fuel. We told him how we had been running on empty for over an hour as each petrol station would only allow us a few litres of fuel before moving us on. He instructed us to bring our truck alongside his tanker, then he attached a filler hose and filled our truck's tank to the top directly from the tanker, only charging us the price displayed on the pump. This enabled us to travel through the rest of the country without being concerned about diesel.

That day I realised again that there are never any shortages in God's Kingdom. No matter what is going on in the world around us, God is more than able to supply whatever we need to fulfil the task He has given us to do. All we need to do is ask Him and then follow His leading and He will meet our need. Many times I have met Christians who have been paralysed in their faith because they are unwilling to move on until they have everything they think they need to complete the task they have been given. Some, having started in faith, come to a halt because they begin to look at the circumstances and fear that God will not provide what they need when they need it, rather than trusting Him. We could have stopped in the town when we were unable to get fuel and prayed while looking at a fuel gauge that registered empty. Some would say that would have been the wise thing to do. But we were seeking to move on to fulfil what God had called us to do and in doing that we met the answer to our prayers and were able to fulfil all that God had called us to accomplish. "And my God will supply all your needs according to His riches in glory."[53]

The roads, on the whole, were in good condition until we came to the highway leading to the border with Bulgaria. This road had some of the biggest potholes I have ever seen anywhere. I felt sure that if a car dropped into one of them it would not be able to continue its journey. Queueing for nearly eleven hours to leave Serbia left us extremely tired.

Being encouraged by most of the other truck drivers that our truck was too small to queue with their juggernauts, we decided to try to go through the smaller vehicle gate where there was no such holdup. This caused somewhat of an uproar with the border guards but we were finally let through after about an hour and we thought

---

[53] Philippians 4:19 (NASB)

we were home free – until we reached the Bulgarian side and realised the Serbs had not given us a piece of paperwork that the Bulgarian border officials insisted we have.

This infraction resulted in our truck being impounded and we had to walk back across no man's land to get the appropriate piece of paper. We were unable to make them understand our request so we rather dejectedly returned to the Bulgarians who were insistent that they would not let us come into their country nor would they let us have our truck back!

We did manage to obtain a photocopy of the requisite paperwork to help us to explain to the Serbians exactly what was needed. However, this backfired big time! The Serbian authorities now accused us of being in possession of forged papers and locked us in a room. Eventually we were led into the Head Border Guard's office. I can only say that her dress resembled that of a stripogram, although I hasten to add, I have no experience in that area! My immediate reaction was that the Serbs were having a joke at our expense because we had passed through the wrong gate and so I naturally started to laugh at the lady stood before me.

This evoked a very strong reaction from the official. I quickly apologised and we were sent back to the Bulgarians but without the papers we needed. On arrival at the checkpoint I asked the guys to pray while I grabbed a large bar of Cadbury's dairy milk chocolate from the cab of the lorry and proceeded to enter the border guard's office once more. I placed the chocolate on her desk and then put my papers on top of it and asked if there was anything she could do to help us in our predicament. She picked up her phone and spoke into the receiver for a few seconds and then retuned the receiver back to its cradle. Stamping our papers, she announced that I was now free to go. I politely enquired whether she was able to accept the chocolate as a 'thank you' gift for her kindness to which she smiled and quickly pocketed the chocolate. "My chains fell off..." I walked out a free man, our truck was released and we drove into Bulgaria a little wiser for our experience and still at least six hours ahead of our fellow truck drivers.

Over the next fifteen miles we were waved over by at least four groups of policemen who, as soon as they spotted an English number plate, saw an opportunity to glean some money from some trumped up fine. Only the first traffic officer succeeded in extorting any money and that was only because I was asleep on the bed behind the driver's seat. I refused subsequent requests for 'fines' to be paid at the roadside by declaring that I did not understand why they wanted money and would need an official receipt. To issue a receipt would necessitate a trip to the local police station and would result in lost opportunities for the officers to supplement their income from other hapless drivers. I have to say these incidents were the exception as most of the people we have met in both Serbia and Bulgaria have been really helpful.

The trip had taken us two-and-a-half days but we had made it across the final border and were now speeding through the night towards Plovdiv, the second largest city in Bulgaria. On the motorway we passed the sign for "McDonalds 20km", a landmark for us as it was the first time we had seen the iconic Golden Arches since leaving the UK. At that precise moment there was a tremendous bang as one of the front tyres exploded and we came to a halt on the hard shoulder, thanking God for keeping us safe and under control even though we had been travelling at speed. We felt sure that the tyre had been damaged by one of the potholes on the Serbian roads leading to the border. A quick phone call brought Craig from Plovdiv to meet us. He took the wheel and spare tyre along with the other drivers to our accommodation. Craig returned the following morning to rescue me with the repaired wheel and we were able to complete our passage on time within the three days we had allowed, praise God! The journey had truly been an adventure but was nothing in comparison with what we were about to experience!

CHAPTER SEVENTEEN

The Gospel with Signs Following

WE MET UP WITH THE REST of our team in a small village in the Plovdiv region. Our accommodation was an ex-communist youth hostel above an animal feed factory. It was quite basic with shared showers and toilets, which meant you had to whistle when in the shower to let the girls know you were ensconced, as the door had no working lock. I discovered that girls talk to each other while in the toilets; most unnerving for the guys on our team! The following day we travelled to the gypsy mahala[54] in Malo Konare where we were planning to site the tent. It concerned me a little as our friend whom we had come to work with didn't seem to know where we were to erect the canvas and we discovered that the permission from the authorities had only been granted a couple of days before we arrived. But, praise God, we soon found the place and a team of very excited gypsies joined us to help put up the tent.

We were all soon learning each other's languages and sharing together. That night surprised us all as over three hundred people turned up to the meeting. The noise in the tent was incredible; you could hardly hear yourself speak even with amplification. The gypsies enjoy their worship loud and took delight in winding the PA up to its limits! The presence of God fell in the tent and from the outset people were getting saved and healed. Every evening the numbers grew. The

---

[54] a term commonly used for the poor minority areas

tent's seating capacity of three hundred and fifty was severely tested one night with nearly seven hundred people squashed in. Again God's presence filled the tent in a very tangible way.

During one meeting a lady came forward who had suffered a stroke. This is quite common among the poorer minorities due to their diet. She was unable to use her arm and dragged her leg badly. We laid hands on her and prayed but nothing discernible appeared to happen. The next morning a man came to me to tell me that the exhaust on my truck had a hole in it and that he was happy to repair the fault if I would drive the vehicle to his house. While he was welding the exhaust pipe he invited me to go into his house and have a coffee with his wife and her mother. To my surprise the mother-in-law was the same lady that we had ministered to the previous evening. Now she was walking normally and shook my hand with the arm that the previous evening was hanging as a dead weight at her side. She told me that when we prayed she felt God moving in her body but nothing visibly changed until the following morning. On waking she found that she had regained total movement in both the affected arm and leg. She grasped my hand to shake it with a vicelike grip. Praise God, she was indeed totally healed!

The Gospel was being preached to the poor with signs following as it had been in New Testament times and hundreds were coming to know Jesus. During the event we spent the mornings together as a team and in the afternoons we spent time with the children teaching them about Jesus and sharing basic hygiene information about washing and cleaning teeth. We played games with the youngsters, seeking to show them the love of God. In the evenings we held Gospel outreach meetings which often did not finish until after midnight due to the large numbers of people getting saved or wanting to receive prayer. The prayer lines seemed to go on forever but God sustained us and all too soon the week was over and we were to move on to the next venue in Saedinenie.

Between these two missions we took a much needed day off and went up into the Rhodope Mountains for a time of relaxation and a little sightseeing. One of our team clearly found the concept of taking time out difficult and spent much of the day by himself making a show of sitting reading his bible. This was OK up to a point but when we were due to move on, Ian was nowhere to be found! Wondering where he might have got to, I looked around and saw market stalls a little way off down the road where there seemed to be no small commotion. Immediately I felt God say, "That's where you'll find him!"

So leaving the rest of the team to get in the minibus, I walked off down the road to the market and, sure enough, there was Ian. He was stood in the middle of a group of twenty-five or so people and was busily praying with a lady. He explained that Father had given him a word of knowledge concerning a lady with a back problem and the woman had let him pray for her and had been instantly healed from her pain. Another lady who had been looking on had asked him to pray for her and now there were twenty-five others waiting for prayer.

Ian turned to me and asked me a question that challenged me to the core: "Are you having a day off or are you going to pray for these sick people?" So I got stuck in ministering alongside him and there in the marketplace we witnessed yet another company of people experience the power of God to heal and set them free.

What my brother Ian said to me that day made me realise that it is so easy for us to box God into working when we feel it is convenient and to miss out on what He might want to do through us at any time in any place. So let me ask you the same question: "Are you having a day off from what God wants you to be doing?"

At this point in the mission I think we all wondered just what God could have in store for us during the second week that could possibly match what had happened during the first! Putting the tent up was a challenge, as the canvas only just fitted on the site at the edge of the mahala, but from the first night God's presence was again very much in evidence and we were privileged to see miracles, healings and people come to know Jesus.

Each evening, as the word went out about what was happening in the tent, the streets were filled with coaches as people travelled in from farther afield.

On the third evening I stepped out into the centre of the tent and knew instantly that the presence of the Holy Spirit had withdrawn from us. Having welcomed everyone, I handed over to the worship group and returned to tell the team what I felt. Everyone concurred that something indeed was very different about the atmosphere. At this point we were in danger of falling into disunity over the reason for this withdrawal of the Spirit's presence as people voiced their differing opinions regarding a course of action.

I decided somewhat apprehensively that the only way ahead was to tell the people that we needed to apologise to the Holy Spirit for whatever we had done to cause Him to leave and to humbly invite Him to return. This we did and once again the presence of God fell in the tent. Later we discovered that the worship leader that evening who had been recommended to us was having an affair with a woman in his church. Even though people had spoken to him about this he had continued to pursue the relationship. We need to always remember that the Holy Spirit is a person and as such can be offended by our actions and might withdraw from us.[55]

The first person that I prayed for that evening was slain in the Spirit and fell to the ground. This was something that the gypsies had not encountered before. To see this lady poleaxed as soon as I touched her as if she had been hit by a two by four was an unnerving experience for them. The following five people in the prayer line fell under the power of the Holy Spirit and I became aware that the large gypsy brother who was helping me was now moving protectively closer to me.

I looked around the crowd and realised that quite a number of people were looking at me in a somewhat menacing fashion. Craig explained that the gypsies suspected that I had actually killed these people as they had never before seen anyone slain in the Spirit. When I looked at those lying on the ground they did all look strangely still and I too began to wonder if indeed they were dead! But, praise God, they started to recover and as the first lady regained her feet, she declared that she had been healed. Once again the atmosphere changed; great joy and excitement became the prevailing mood and a sticky situation was averted!

The following night I felt that God wanted to focus on the men, very few of whom had come forward for salvation. Roma men are very much like English men in that they have a culture of pride and are often unwilling to respond in any meeting. They fear being seen as weak. As I preached I grew in confidence, knowing that indeed God

---

[55] See Ephesians 4:30

wanted men to come and have their lives changed. I almost burst into tears when I made the appeal and between forty and fifty men came forward, some weeping as they responded to the altar call. It was a fantastic sight and heralded a breakthrough into something new in the Spirit.

The next day we were scheduled to be teaching the leaders on healing but as there was work in the fields no one turned up for the teaching! This was not because anyone had taken offence but rather that in communities where they live from hand to mouth often there is very little available work. When work does present itself it needs to be taken. God had another plan to demonstrate that He has made us all part of a Kingdom of priests.[56] As there were a number of the teenagers hanging around the tent, we sat them down and taught them the material instead.

That evening there were more people than ever at the crusade as coaches arrived from the surrounding villages. I noticed one boy being carried into the meeting as his legs appeared like rubber with no strength in them and they appeared to bend in places where legs really should not! His wheelchair was pushed across the rough ground behind him and then he was lowered into it as he took his place in the tent. I was reminded of the account of the paralyzed man and his friends in Mark 2:3.

The tent was so full that we had to take the side walls down so that people could overflow outside. Again we worshipped, preached the Gospel and people got saved. When it came to the time to pray for the sick I felt God tell me to release the teenagers we had taught that afternoon. In having them pray for the sick it would demonstrate that it is all believers who are meant to minister healing[57] not just white people from England or leaders in the church. This was not a very popular decision amongst the people and they pushed forward for us to pray as we had done before. While we were ministering I became aware of a Mexican wave of applause that had started over to my left which grew and flowed around the tent. I could not see what had caused this as people were pressing in all around. Then I caught sight of the boy who had been carried in and put in the

---

[56] See Revelation 1:6
[57] See Mark 16:17

wheelchair; he was now standing and walking around the tent with no help at all!

Later on I discovered that when the teenagers we had taught that afternoon were released to pray, they had headed straight for the boy and healed him in Jesus' name. When I asked them what they had done they told me hesitantly, "We only did what you taught us this afternoon!"

Earlier that day I had recounted to them the story of Smith Wigglesworth who, when standing before a man in a wheelchair, had felt God tell him to tell the stricken man to stand and immediately had heard another voice ask, "What happens when he doesn't?"

To this Wigglesworth replied by dragging the man from his chair and commanding him to stand, and then said, "What happens to you now, Satan, now that he is standing?"

Having heard this, these young men and women had gone to their friend, dragged him from his chair and commanded him to walk, which he immediately did and was completely healed. If only we all moved in that simple level of faith. They heard that God had healed a man in a wheelchair and thought that if He did it through Wigglesworth He would do it through them, and their faith was rewarded, praise God!

I was reminded once more that evening that power is held in a testimony. Now whenever I hear of God doing things elsewhere that I have not yet seen I pray, "Lord, if you did it there I know that You don't love them any more than You love me and the people I am ministering to – so please do those things amongst us as well."

We were so blessed by our two weeks in Bulgaria. It far exceeded our wildest expectations. I lost count of the many people who were saved, healed, filled with the Holy Spirit and spoke in other tongues. In addition to what was happening in the evenings, many children made Jesus their Lord during the Kids Clubs in the afternoons. And to think that we could have missed out on all of this! The number of times that I was tempted to give up and not go as I listened to all the negative things we were being told while preparing! It would have been so easy to persuade myself that I had not really heard God because it was so difficult. But then we would have missed out on everything that God had planned for us. It is so important once you hear the Lord call you to a course of action to keep your eyes fixed on Him. When Peter was responding to Jesus' call to come to Him walking on the water[58] it was only as he looked away from Jesus and saw the wind and the waves that fear entered his heart and he started to sink. You see, at that point his natural wisdom kicked in. He was a fisherman and he knew about the wind and waves; he saw something that caused him to be afraid and that fear overcame his faith. He was already walking on the water, doing the impossible, yet fear caused him to sink. You see, fear and faith are opposites and the devil seeks to sow fear into our hearts because it undermines our faith.

On the three-day journey home there were only two of us to drive, as our other driver had only been able to do the downward leg and we had been unable to find anyone else to help. But, praise God, it went fairly uneventfully apart from one or two small queues at the borders. During the long days driving home God encouraged me that because we were faithful and did what He had asked of us, He would open up doors for us to minister in every one of the ten nations we had driven through. I am reminded of that old English saying that from little acorns mighty oak trees grow. As we step through the doors that God opens to us, we can never be sure just where they will take us. At times they may seem insignificant but God loves to reward us when we move out in faith and do what He has asked of us.

---

[58] See Matthew 14:28

Chapter Eighteen

Obedience Opens Doors

I WAS AT OUR NETWORK'S annual conference at Hothorpe Hall in Leicestershire when, on the last evening, the housekeeping team asked us to take the bed linen from our beds in the morning, fold it and leave it outside our rooms. I'm not a modern man and, as such, not used to folding sheets. I considered the request to be crazy as someone would have to unfold the linen to put it in the washing machine! So I left mine in a pile outside the room and, glancing along the corridor at several untidy heaps of duvet covers and sheets, could see that I was not alone in my thinking!

I took my place in the conference hall and as the first seminar was about to start, God asked me, "How can you expect Me to trust you with great things when you cannot even submit to the housekeeper's request?"

I tried to argue my point but you know that it is a losing battle as God always wins. I jumped up and ran to my room hoping that the linen had not yet been collected. Praise God, it was still there. I took my time and folded the linen perfectly and left it in a neat pile outside the room exactly as requested. Then I returned to the tail end of the first teaching session wondering just what all that was about.

Some months later I was preaching in a church about the Kingdom of God being at hand which meant that it was so close we could reach out and take hold of it. At the end of the meeting we were praying with people and a lady came forward who had been diagnosed with lung cancer. She was waiting for a second scan to help the doctors decide what course of treatment was appropriate for her tumour. As I was praying for her, I heard Father God tell me, "In My Kingdom there is a new pair of lungs for her," to which I replied, "Yes, I know."

Father then told me to reach out and take them and give them to her.

I asked Him, "Just how do I do that?"

The Lord told me to close my eyes. In my mind I could see a pair of lungs inflating and deflating, and He said, "There they are; give them to her."

"But they're in my mind, Lord!"

Father replied, "No, they're in my Kingdom and because you folded the bed linen I will allow you to reach into my Kingdom and take them and give them to this lady."

I assured the lady that in God's Kingdom there was a new pair of lungs for her and I reached out my arm and took hold of what appeared to be thin air and then placed my hand on the lady saying, "Here you are. Have your new lungs."

She looked at me very strangely and quickly went back to her seat. A few days later she phoned and told me that she had just returned from the second scan and the doctors could not find any cancer in her lungs. She relayed to me how the doctor had said something that prompted her to ring me; when he looked at the two scans he puzzled, "This is strange; it doesn't even look like you have the same pair of lungs." At that point she remembered what I had told her that Sunday evening.

I have recounted this story many times and one evening after sharing the tale two guys came up to me independently. Both had been at the conference where God had told me to go back and fold the linen. Both had felt like me that the housekeeper's request was crazy. Both had been in the conference hall and heard God say, "Go back and fold the linen." Both had ignored that still small voice. Now both were looking rather crestfallen and wondering just what God would have allowed them to do if they had folded their linen.

I believe that God will only give us authority to the measure at which we are willing to submit to the authorities He has placed in our lives. We are called to submit to all authorities, not just God's direct authorities.[59] We should seek to submit to the Word of God, to our leaders in the church, to governments and the laws of the land and, yes, even to ladies who ask us to fold our linen. More than that, we are called to pray for them.

As you read the Bible, you can see that this principle even worked in the life of our Lord. When the centurion came to Jesus, the Roman made a statement that revealed that he had noticed something about Jesus that no one else had realized about Him. Many had asked by what authority the carpenter's son did what He did, by whose authority He was working. The centurion discerned that Jesus was a man who was under authority and, recognizing this, he knew full well that He must also be a man *with* authority; that He could just say the word and the centurion's servant would be made well.[60] Time and again Jesus declared himself to be living under His Father's authority.[61]

There is another principle that is found throughout the Bible that is very closely linked to this one. It is simply that if you are faithful in small things, God will release you into greater things. This is seen in the parable of the talents.[62] The Master rewarded those who were faithful with what had been entrusted to them by putting them in charge of even more. This same code can be seen in the lives of David and Joseph plus numerous other biblical figures. Many people have great callings but are less than willing to serve in the smaller things that God puts before them. One of the very first areas in which I was asked to serve as a young Christian was to fill the baptistery and then to empty it again once the meeting was over. It took some four hours to fill the pool, which wasn't too onerous as you could turn the valve on and then simply return three-and-a-half hours later to a full tank. But emptying the baptistery was a whole different ball game! That process took the best part of six hours because the pump had to be piped to an outside drain and it could not be left as the door to the church needed to be propped open. So you had to remain there. This was in the days before I could read properly so with no distraction it seemed like a lifetime!

---

[59] See Romans 13:1
[60] See Matthew 8:5
[61] See, for example, Luke 10:22 and John 12:49
[62] See Matthew 25:14

To my amazement one Sunday morning, the guy whom I was meant to be helping with this task but who rarely put in an appearance was announced as the deacon in charge of such duties. My initial reaction was, "I do all the work and he gets all the recognition!"

God very graciously spoke to me the next time that I found myself sat in an empty building after a baptismal service: "I see that you are being faithful and it is I who will open doors that no man can close. Continue in being faithful and I will reward you."

Father reminded of when Samuel anointed David.[63] In man's eyes this young man was the last choice but God had other ideas. We need to put our trust in God to fulfil all His promises to us because if we start to look to other sources to bring about our godly ambitions we could well end up disappointed. If we put our hope in God, no matter what man does, God will ensure that His purposes are fulfilled. Think about David; he was anointed to be king yet for a while he continued as a shepherd. Even when he was called to serve in Saul's house, it was not all it might have been as Saul tried to kill him! Yet David continued to be faithful, and God looked after him and at the right time brought him to the place to fulfil all that the young shepherd boy had been promised.

The same was true of Joseph. He had a dream which got him into all sorts of trouble and his brothers wanted to kill him. They relented and sold him into slavery, yet because he was faithful in the small responsibilities that came his way, whether it was in Potiphar's house or in prison, he was promoted to a place of authority and eventually fulfilled his God-given dream. If God has given you dreams, if He has promised you great things, keep serving faithfully in the small things and He will fulfil all that He intends for you regardless of what man may say or do. This is a God-given principle that will not fail you. If you find that you are not progressing at the pace you think you should be, it might be worth asking yourself, "Am I being faithful in the small things that God has given me to do or have I become distracted?"

---

[63] See 1 Samuel 16:11

CHAPTER NINETEEN

Forgiveness and Healing Flow

THINGS WERE GOING WELL IN THE UK and soon after our return home from Bulgaria we started our mission season working with churches throughout the south of England. We were beginning to see many more healings in these events. One man came for prayer as he had lost all the feeling in his legs as a result of a kidney problem. When I started to pray for him I felt God tell me that there was more to this than met the eye. So I started to gently question him about the circumstances of the kidney failure. He recounted how the onset of symptoms had coincided with his daughter leaving home after many disputes and that several years later he had no contact with her at all. It was clear that there was some level of unforgiveness on his part. I counselled him that he needed to forgive her as Christ had indeed forgiven him and to seek to restore the relationship. That night he went home and phoned his daughter and asked for her forgiveness for the things he had said and done. There was a tearful reunion on the phone with forgiveness on both sides. There was still more good news when he awoke the next morning and found that he had regained complete feeling in his legs once again. He had responded positively to the word God had given him through me.

Sadly, I also experienced the flip side. While ministering in Sri Lanka a man came forward for prayer for a withered hand. I can only describe the limb as having the appearance of the claws of a bird of prey; the arm was thin and twisted and he had very little use in it. My friend Charles and I laid our hands on his withered limb and commanded it to be made whole. When we took our hands away the hand was as it should be and the guy now had full use of it. As we started to praise God for the wonderful miracle we had just seen, the hand twisted and returned to its previous state before our very eyes! Both Charles and I were shocked by what we had witnessed and felt sure that the devil was stealing this man's healing and health. So, determined to pray again, we laid our hands on the withered hand and commanded it to be whole. When we removed our hands the arm was once again restored and functioning. However, after a few minutes, once more, it twisted and returned to its previous state. We were perplexed by this and felt sure that there was demonic activity that was hindering this man's healing. So for a third time we laid hands on the affected limb and also bound any demonic being that was opposing the work of the Spirit. We loosed the power of God to bring about healing and once more when we removed our hands the arm was whole again and remained that way for several minutes. Then, to our frustration, yet again it twisted and returned to its previous state.

By now neither of us were sure quite what to do so we did what all believers should – we asked Jesus! As we did this, a vision came to me of a path not unlike one you might see anywhere in rural Sri Lanka. This path ran down between two pieces of land. I had no idea what this meant so I initially dismissed it and continued praying, but the picture would not go away and so I shared the vision with the man and asked if it meant anything to him.

He started to cry and told us of when his father had died and had bequeathed his lands to his three sons. The best parcel of land had been willed to this man standing before us as he was the favourite son. However, it was completely surrounded by his two brothers' land and the only access to his land was along a path that passed through theirs. The brothers were refusing him access until he agreed to share the parcel of land so that each one of them received part of the good land. He was refusing to submit to this request and had been to court to try to force his brothers to give him access but had failed. Now he was very bitter and holding much unforgiveness. I felt sure that God had revealed this because it was the cause of his inability to hold onto his healing and I counselled him that he needed to forgive his brothers to receive what God wanted to give him. He looked at me sadly and told me that he would never be able to forgive his brothers for their course of action. He turned and walked away.

We can see from this that it is God's desire to heal and indeed three times God showed this man His intent. Each time unforgiveness was the wedge that left the door open for the devil to oppress him once again. The Bible encourages us not to let the "sun go down on your anger"[64] because in doing so we give the devil a foothold. Unresolved anger can so easily turn to unforgiveness and that unforgiveness can be a block to us from entering into all that God has planned for us: life in abundance.[65]

Unforgiveness can even open the door to sickness. I have experienced this first-hand. I had enjoyed a ministry trip to Vietnam where Derek and I had been teaching at the New Life Fellowship of Churches' annual leaders' conference. This drew leaders from churches all around South East Asia. It was an amazing time to be working in this Asian Communist nation where Christians were still much persecuted. One day we took some time out and walked along the seafront where we came upon a massive statue of Jesus with his arms spread wide. It was so big that there was a doorway in His foot that led to stairs that enabled you to climb up inside Jesus and walk out on His outstretched arms. The statue overlooking Vung Tau city is over thirty meters high. It reminded us of the scripture in John 14:20 where Jesus declares that "on that day you will realise that I am in my Father and you are in Me and I am in you". Here we were climbing up in Jesus yet He is in us. It really impacted us that this is how the world should see us; we are hidden in Jesus yet He is in us. TL Osbourne, the great evangelist, used to often say, "You are the only Jesus some people will ever see."

On my return home, I was struck down with what appeared to be some type of tropical infection. It initially manifested itself when my knee joint gave out as I was coming down our stairs at home, causing me to fall the rest of the way. Praise God, I was not hurt, and put it down to clumsiness until a couple of days later when it happened again. This was quickly followed by considerable loss of use of my hands. Simple tasks such as trying to pick up a piece of paper and not

---

[64] Ephesians 4:26b (NASB)
[65] See John 10:10

being able to close my fingers to do so kept me busy for many minutes! After numerous trips to the doctor and many blood tests, the situation continued to deteriorate to the point where all of my joints were being affected and I seriously began to wonder if I was to become a cripple for the rest of my days. Some mornings I could hardly walk and most days I needed the aid of a walking stick which presented great difficulty as my hands were reluctant to co-operate! My doctor prescribed a course of steroids to protect my joints from permanent damage while they continued investigations to determine the cause of the problem. My health was in steady decline and I was becoming increasingly debilitated.

While at a conference a friend, Martin, approached me and asked if he could pray for me. I had been confessing the Word and receiving prayer as often as I could. I had put my trust in my Lord to cause my healing to be made manifest in my body and happily received the opportunity to receive more prayer. He had only prayed over me for a few seconds when he took his hand away and told me that he thought that I was holding unforgiveness in my heart which was the cause of my sickness. I had to admit that this was true. Certain events had happened and various things had been said about me which were untrue. I found it difficult to believe that the hurt these incidences provoked was unintentional. I had decided that the best course of action was to simply avoid the person in question but deep inside there was this unforgiveness festering. I knew that it was there and had tried to deal with it but I was unable to let go of the fact that I thought there was an agenda behind what had been said which had discredited me and so I had wanted nothing to do with this person. I could see no way of forgiving them.

Now here I was being told that this was the cause of my sickness. I had to admit that I had become entrenched in my position and didn't want to forgive even if I could find a way of doing it and getting beyond the bitterness. My friend asked me a simple question: "Is it worth being sick over?" He reminded me that my unforgiveness was only causing me harm and not the person who was the object of it. This, of course, was true but I still had a problem; I did not know how to let go of it. Every time in the past when I had tried to 'give it over to the Lord', within a few days it was there again festering and causing me pain. I was living with the consequences of what had been said and done. My friend suggested that we ask God for the answer to the problem so I reluctantly prayed along those lines. We had not even said "amen" when we were joined by another brother asking us to come and pray for someone who had just put their back out and was now lying on the floor waiting for an ambulance to come to take them to hospital. I guess you know who it was lying on the floor – the person I could not forgive. I had a choice in that moment; forgive and start praying for the person or hold on to all that resentment. I chose to pray for him, and with each passing day that I prayed for his wellbeing more use returned to my body, so much so that within a couple of weeks I had no sign of the sickness which had laid me low for so many months. Even now I choose to pray for them rather than think ill of them whenever those thoughts come back as they do from time to time. Yongi Cho once said, "A bird can land on your head but you don't have to let it build a nest." We can't stop negative thoughts coming into our minds but we don't have to dwell on them, we need to take them captive. When Paul wrote to the Corinthians he encouraged them to take every thought that is raised up against the knowledge of God captive to the obedience of Christ.[66] That is, every thought that is differing from Christ-centered thinking; we should take hold of such notions and replace them with godly attitudes. This causes our souls to prosper and a prosperous soul causes our whole being to do well and be in health in every area of our lives.[67]

While all this was going on Kim had been diagnosed with a problem in both her ears which was causing her to have a significant loss of hearing and she had been fitted with two hearing aids. On top of this the doctors had discovered that one of her eardrums was completely in shreds and that she required an operation to replace it. We had often prayed about this situation over the years but nothing appeared to improve; in fact, it just seemed to get worse which was a challenge to our faith especially as we were seeing God do so much through us in other people. Eventually Kim attended an appointment with the hospital for pre-op checks and was told that the surgeon would remove a small piece of muscle from behind her ear and use it to replace the damaged ear drum, a procedure known as a myringoplasty. This, they told her, would probably not improve her

---

[66] See 2 Corinthians 10:5
[67] See 3 John 2

120

hearing but would help prevent ear infections which were becoming an increasing problem. The week she was due to go in for the operation she received a second letter asking her to attend the clinic again for pre-op checks. Kim phoned the hospital to check that this duplication was not a mistake and was told no, she needed to come in.

At this time, I was involved in our Year Out Bible School which our son Tom was attending. The subject I was teaching that week was that we are all anointed to move in healing power. When we returned home that evening our son, fired up by the day's teaching, announced that he did not believe that it was God's best for his mum to have to go into hospital for the operation and that he would like to pray with her, which he did there and then. Nothing appeared to change and two days later Kim went for the second set of pre-op checks.

On arrival at the hospital, the receptionist asked her what she was doing there again and she explained how she had received the second letter and been told to come in. The perplexed lady replied that it must have been a mistake but as Kim had come all this way they would check her again. When she went in to see one of the doctors he examined her ear with a small telescope and announced that he needed to get a second opinion. At his invitation, a second doctor came and looked in her ear and then they called the consultant in and all three of them examined her ear yet again. The consultant then told Kim that they would not be performing the operation after all.

When Kim asked, "But, why?" the consultant placed a small camera in her ear to show her a perfectly intact, pink eardrum. In front of him were Kim's notes complete with a picture of a tattered membrane. His comment was that he couldn't explain what had happened in the interval between appointments!

As she took her leave one of the junior doctors thanked Kim for "letting me look in your ear, I've never seen anything like that before!" to which the consultant added, "And you probably never will again." Over the next few weeks Kim started to complain when we were watching TV that it was too loud, something she had never done before, and so the TV got turned down to a more acceptable level for the rest of the family. Yet she still complained it was too loud and eventually it was so quiet that the rest of us were beginning to question our own hearing abilities! I suggested that she remove her hearing aids, which she did, and to all of our amazement was able to hear almost normally.

That day when our son prayed for her, a creative miracle took place and an eardrum came into existence. Such is the goodness of God that that same healing power began a work to restore her hearing. Today, there is still room for improvement in her hearing and we continue to believe God that He is going to complete the work that He has started.[68] At this time she no longer uses hearing aids and we are so grateful to God because the original medical prognosis was that she would eventually completely lose her hearing. All through this experience Kim refused to accept this prognosis and would receive prayer whenever the opportunity arose, and despite seeing her hearing decline over a period of ten years, our persistence brought about the breakthrough when Tom obeyed Father's prompting and laid hands on his mother.[69] I want to encourage you to never give up on God's promises as He is always faithful to fulfil them if we continue to put our faith and trust in Him.

---

[68] See Philippians 1:6
[69] See Luke 11:5

CHAPTER TWENTY

Salvations and Miracles

THE DIRECTION THAT MY LIFE and ministry was taking resulted in me spending ever increasing amounts of time travelling as I sought to fulfil all that I felt God was calling me to do. The mission work in Bulgaria was continuing to have an impact on my diary as I was now being asked to return to help train leaders to care for the people who had come to know Jesus during our outreach events in this Balkan nation. I started to travel there three or four times a year accompanied by Kim as well as by two friends Martin and Steve.

During these trips the healings and the miracles continued. During one of these visits, along with the local leaders, we felt that God was calling us to hold a mission in one of the gypsy areas in the centre of Plovdiv, which is the second largest city in Bulgaria. Previously we had only worked in gypsy areas on the outskirts of the city. We felt that we could plant a significant church in that area where there was in excess of some seventy thousand gypsies and no recognised churches. We liaised with the other churches that bordered the area and most agreed to support the mission, and plans were set in motion to again bring the tent to Bulgaria. We would bring an extra section so that we could seat fifteen hundred people. As I mentioned previously, I was at this time teaching on a course back home for people from churches around our area who had taken a year off to study and serve in the local congregations. It was agreed that the culmination of the course would be this mission trip. The students were to be joined by others from another church in the UK called Living Waters in Clevedon, North Somerset.

So in the May of 2006 our two Spearhead trucks with a team of six drivers set out for Bulgaria carrying our tent and all its equipment. The rest of the team flew down to Sofia and rendezvoused with the tent and equipment in Plovdiv. We were joined by a team of young men from Tajikistan who had come to perform breakdance. Our team numbered over thirty of varying ages, a significant increase in number from the previous year. The tent went up and from the first evening of the ten-night crusade our expectations were met and exceeded as hundreds of gypsies gathered in the tent. The noise was incredible as everyone was very excited! Earplugs are requisite equipment for all mission team members!

The presence of God was tangible and after the word was preached every evening we would pray for people late into the night and return to the hotel exhausted. During the day we met as a team and prayed and then arrived at the tent to run sports clubs, breakdancing lessons and children's ministry. The tent was full of excitement, both from the team and from those they were ministering to. Each evening we worshipped God, heard testimonies and preached the Gospel and every night people were saved and healed.

We started to draw the attention of the local Muslim population as night after night people were giving their lives to Jesus. A group of young men arrived to disrupt the meetings and they cut the tent and PA cables and threatened the stewards. One evening while I was preaching one of our stewards was dragged from the back of the tent and was set upon by a group. They had taken exception to the way that he had asked a group of young boys to leave the tent. It was as if a fight had broken out in a school yard! "Fight, fight, fight!" Most of the thousand plus people in the tent got up out of their seats and left to see what was happening outside.

When you are in the middle of your word and your congregation run out it does rather leave you wondering at the quality of your delivery! I asked God, "What shall I do?" and felt Him reply, "There is a lady here in the tent who is blind in one eye."

I looked out over the much reduced crowd of a hundred or so folk and tried to spot the woman who might be blind. I knew for certain that thirty of them were definitely not blind as they made up our team! I asked God, "Are You sure, Lord? I can't see anyone."

At the same time, I was being pressured by the local leaders to bring the worship band back onto the stage to try to draw everybody back into the tent. God told me, "I can see her!" and so I spoke out, "Is there a lady here who is blind in one eye?"

To my amazement a woman stood up and came forward. She was clearly blind in her left eye. I started to pray for her and, as has become my custom, I asked Father, "How should I do this?" to which He replied, "Lay your hand over the blind eye."

I obeyed His instruction and then asked, "What next?"

"Tell her that she is healed." Which I did.

Looking for the next step, I asked, "What now?"

"Take your hand away."

To which my reply was, "It can't be that easy!" and left my hand covering her eye.

Father graciously encouraged me with, "You will never know if she is healed until you take your hand away!"

I realised that I was beginning to look rather silly just standing there with my hand covering the lady's eye so, with a large gulp, I gathered up my trust in God and took my hand away. The woman screamed out, "I can see!"

Everybody who had left the tent heard her shout and they all came running back in to see the miracle. They brought others with them and I continued to preach the Good News to an even larger, very attentive crowd.

As I was speaking, I was interrupted by a lady who could hardly walk, struggling to the front of the meeting. She had witnessed the healing that had just taken place and wanted God to touch her as well. My interpreter relayed her history of how she had fallen from a third storey window (many of the windows in the decrepit blocks of flats surrounding the tent had lost their glazing) and broken her hip and legs. After some considerable time in hospital she had been released with her walking very badly impaired.

As I laid hands on her I felt God tell me, "Run with her to the other side of the tent."

We set off and she stumbled along and fell. I waited for her and we started off again. Bless her, she stumbled and fell again and I helped her back to her feet. A third time we started to run and this time we made it to the end of the tent, some one hundred and thirty feet in all, and when she touched the canvas she turned and ran back at breakneck speed to where we had started. Completely healed, her gait returned to normal, she walked back into the congregation whole. Praise God!

Later that evening two young men who were part of our team, Kevin and Tom, called me over to see a young boy they had just prayed with. The boy was standing there answering questions being put to him which didn't seem particularly remarkable! I asked the lads, "What am I supposed to be looking at?"

They told me how the boy had been deaf and dumb a few moments before. I must admit, I was a little sceptical as I thought that perhaps the boy was simply shy in speaking to these Englishmen. I looked up to see a lady standing behind the youngster who was weeping copiously. On enquiring the reason for her tears, she replied that this was the first time she had ever heard her son speak and could see that he could now hear as he was answering questions being put to him.

Three miracles had taken place in the young boy's body: his hearing had been restored; he had spoken for the first time; and the Spirit had 'downloaded' the Bulgarian language into him all in a matter of moments. No wonder his mother was overwhelmed by tears of joy!

During this event we were invited into the local mayor's office as he wished to speak with us. On our arrival, he explained that he had been told about what was happening at the tent. He informed us that the locale we were working in was notorious as a problem area. It consisted of marginalized people, some ninety per cent of whom were of the Muslim persuasion. The authorities had been working for five years to make an impact on the heart of the community with no success. This was surprising news to us as we were under the impression that the area was only thirty per cent Muslim.

It was being reported to the mayor that in the five days we had been on site we had made major inroads into the community and he was interested in learning just how we had managed to impact the people. This gave us a great opportunity to share our faith with him! The mayor promised to help us in any way he could to find a building for our new church to meet in. We returned to the tent overjoyed at this wonderful opening.

The advance of the Kingdom is often contested, and the activity of the enemy continued during the crusade. One evening our PA speakers broke, making it difficult to be heard, but God has blessed me with a loud voice and enabled me to overcome the hubbub which always accompanies the crowds of easily excitable gypsies and we continued to see people saved.

The next evening my preaching was again interrupted as a girl was carried into the tent on a stretcher. She had fallen from a fourth floor window a few minutes before and was clearly in some distress. They had seen the lady who had suffered the same catastrophe healed a few nights before and had insisted on bringing their friend to the tent for prayer before allowing her to be taken to the hospital. They were looking for a better outcome than that of medical intervention which they had seen previously. We prayed for this girl and then gave them a little money to enable them to take her to the hospital to be checked out. The following day the girl returned to the tent to report that the doctors had found nothing whatsoever damaged and had released her. There was much praise to God!

We saw, on average, some thirty people each day make decisions to follow Christ. On the last day of the event I purchased a metre-deep, rigid plastic pool and we baptised around eighty-five people there in the tent. It was awesome to hear these new brothers and sisters confess Jesus as Lord of their lives in front of their Muslim neighbours, the very same people who had tried so hard to close us down.

We had experienced a level of opposition, and the tent and our equipment bore the scars to prove it. But our God is greater than all the works of the enemy and the Gospel prevailed.[70] A church was planted and still meets in the middle of the community there in Izgrev. We launched a football team which teaches the young lads discipline and encourages them to attend school and keep away from the drugs and gangs in the community. These young men are actively encouraged to make Jesus Lord of their lives, which many of them have continued to do since the mission.

---

[70] See 1 John 4:4

Segun along with his wife Joanna now lead this church. Segun grew up in the slums in Nigeria with a talent for playing football. This skill brought him to Bulgaria to play professional football for one of the local clubs in Plovdiv until he suffered a knee injury which abruptly ended his career. Segun offered to serve our team by helping with sports activities as his background uniquely qualified him to work with the young people from this mahala. It soon became clear that he had much more gifting than just working with young people and we approached him to co-ordinate the follow up work as the number of responses during the mission was overwhelming. Ultimately this led to Segun pastoring the new fledgling church, which has continued to grow over the years. In addition to the church, he has birthed a number of football teams.

The mission team returned home as Craig and I set off with the trucks on the return journey. We stopped in Serbia and started to fulfil the word God had given me on the return journey from our initial visit to the Balkans: that we would preach in every one of the ten countries we had travelled through. Another team of eight joined us from King's Church Epsom and we worked with a group of Serbian churches in Backi Petrovac headed up by Miro Fic, a Slovakian evangelist living in Serbia. The smallest tent only just fitted on the site set aside for the event and it required some very careful positioning of the marquee, and even then some of the guy ropes had to be anchored on the other side of a small stream that ran through the plot!

Now the tent was up in a different country with people of different customs. I was politely informed not to expect these people to come forward in response to the Gospel message. Yet every night they walked forward and into new life in Jesus and to receive healing. One evening we encouraged the team of Epsom young people to seek God for words of knowledge and every one of them had a word and had someone respond so that they were able to pray for them. The following night I encouraged the local believers to step out in the gifts of the Spirit and one sister stepped up with a word concerning someone with a skin complaint. A young lady responded and had what appeared to be a purple birthmark which covered her arms and other parts of her body. We all watched in amazement as the sister prayed with the girl and the purple marking faded and disappeared!

She visited the ladies' room to check the rest of her body and returned to report that all the blemishes had disappeared.

A smaller number of people responded for salvation during our time in Serbia but I am conscious of how differing people groups respond in differing ways to God and indeed in differing time frames. Praise God for the ones who did get saved and healed and added to the churches!

On our last night in Serbia we were invited over the border, some fifty miles away, to minister at a meeting with a church in Osijek in Croatia, which was a great time with God and the church. This visit opened the door for us to return there the following year with the tent to support the Word of Life church headed up by Slavko and Mauritsa and its work in their outreach programme.

Since then we have held many tent missions in both of these nations with great success.

Praise God! He is faithful to whatever He tells us and continues to open doors in the nations where He has promised that I will preach the Gospel.

Chapter Twenty-One

Seed to Sow and Bread to Eat

ALL THIS TRAVELLING RESULTED IN Kim and I spending less and less time together as she was working full time in a local school and we could not manage without her salary. With limited administrative support, I would often find myself organising the next mission by email while ministering at another crusade; not an easy task, never mind the pressures on time and my organizational skills! I very much felt that my lack of time was, in effect, putting a stop on further areas that Father wanted me to work in.

It became clear that something had to change; I needed more consistent support in admin which was a bigger part of Kim's role in school and we realised that we needed to spend more time together. We started to pray for extra income to release her to come and work with me.

Two years went by and we saw no extra finance come in, yet the difficulties only seemed to grow and the resulting limitations became increasingly frustrating. One weekend in the spring of 2006, Ian Andrews was staying with us as he had come to minister to the healing teams we had trained and gathered from around the country. As we were sitting over breakfast, Ian paused and then said, "I believe God wants to meet all your needs."

So I asked him if God had said anything in particular to which he replied, "No, just any needs you have." I related to him how we had been praying for the money to be released so Kim could come to work with me, to which he declared, "Well, it's not a need."

Shocked, I protested, "Yes, it is!"

Ian very wisely explained that while Kim still had a salary coming in we had no need. That night Kim and I talked through what Ian had counselled and agreed that on Monday morning she would give in her notice at work and finish at the Easter break, some six weeks away.

No sooner had she tended her resignation than we received a gift of a thousand pounds from Kenneth Copeland Ministries. This of course was nowhere near the total sum that was needed to make up the shortfall and although we were very encouraged we both felt that it was in fact seed money.

The Scripture tells us that God gives us seed to sow and bread to eat.[71] It is so important that we don't eat that which we are meant to sow, otherwise there is no harvest to come in the future. Within a couple of days, it became clear to us where we were to sow this money and we were able to set aside the funds to buy a motorbike for a pastor in Uganda named Joel, to help him visit his more rural churches, and money for a keyboard for a church in Malo Konare in Bulgaria. As the weeks went by, no more money came in but we were sure that God had promised to meet all our needs and at this point we didn't yet have any as Kim was still working out her notice period.

The first thing we planned to do after Kim came to work with me was to take a team on a mission to Kampala in Uganda and so we booked the air tickets for the week she finished work. The week before our departure we received a cheque for two thousand pounds from a trust which sponsors evangelistic works. They had heard about our work in Serbia and were keen to support us. By the time we left for Africa we had received enough money to cover her salary for the next year plus travelling expenses. Our church also pledged to give an annual amount, a great blessing! Each subsequent year her salary has continued to be covered and God has met whatever needs we have had. You see, God's words are always true. Sometimes they require us to step out of our comfort zone and into the faith realm

---

[71] See 2 Corinthians 9:10

before we can receive all that He has promised. Having a wise counsel speak into your life is rather helpful too! That's why we are to listen to each other.[72]

How did we come to be travelling to Kampala? I had received an email from Africa, one of many I get from the third world. Most of these communications are seeking money for various projects, not all of which are very godly! So, as I had done many times before, I deleted the email. As I was walking out of my office, God clearly said to me, "You didn't even read that one."

I know God well enough to know that when He speaks there is always good reason and so I returned to my desk, 'undeleted' the email and sat down to read it. To my surprise there was no request for money, just an invitation to go to minister in Uganda. Still feeling very cautious, I replied to the email, asking some questions about who they were and what they wanted.

The subsequent reply indicated that this church had heard of us by a roundabout route and of our work in Bulgaria, and the congregation in Kampala had been praying for us for the last year or so. They now felt that the time had come to invite us to minister in their small church in a suburb of the Ugandan capital. Feeling that God had promoted this request to me, we made arrangements to travel with a small team to minister to this Ugandan church.

After a long and fairly arduous journey we were not sure what to expect or indeed if there would be anyone there to greet us at the airport. I do not think that anything could have prepared us for the welcome we were about to receive. As we walked from the arrivals lounge we were met by a large group of people from the church all dressed in colourful national costume, dancing in welcome. They had arrived complete with local drinks and snacks for us. They told us that they were not even sure if we were coming as on a number of occasions people had arranged to visit them and they had turned up to greet them at the airport only to be disappointed when no one arrived. They realised they had been the butt of some sort of sick joke. What joy there was on both sides as we met in the terminal at Entebbe Airport.

---

[72] See Proverbs 27:9, 12:15, 13:10

The next part of our journey from the airport to the centre of Kampala was to introduce us to one of the less desirable forms of transport in Africa – the local minibuses, most of which had very little meaningful suspension or shock absorbers. These are generally driven at high speed on roads which often are little more than dirt tracks with potholes everywhere. The drivers' modus operandi is that you have to overtake everything you can see in front of you no matter what may be coming the other way. Much to our consternation they seemed to delight in attempting to pass through the narrowest of gaps in the heavy traffic.

Eventually we made it to our hotel without being involved in any major traffic incident. The hotel was basic but clean and tidy which we were all grateful for. It was sadly on the opposite side of Kampala to where the church met and the conference and healing crusade was planned to take place. This meant that we had to run the gauntlet of Kampala traffic for a couple of hours every day in our minibuses. Breakfast at the hotel was always fun and became a bit of a joke. Every morning we were offered the choice of eggs for our breakfast. The waiter would read from a list of what was available: fried, poached, scrambled, soft or hard boiled. But no matter what you asked for, and which he carefully wrote down, we always got the same: hard boiled eggs. Yet everyday he insisted on going through the same charade, much to our amusement.

We spoke to leaders from a number of small churches during the daytime in a large oven which they called a "church building". Mud walls, a corrugated tin roof and little ventilation made for very high temperatures. In the evenings we ministered at both church meetings and a number of open-air outreach gatherings.

During one of the afternoon meetings where we had been teaching on moving in the power of the Holy Spirit, Kim brought a young girl called Mombasa Dora to me. Dora was a girl of around ten years of age, one of the many AIDS orphans in the slum community of Wabigalo, and she was a cripple from birth. She had one knee joint that simply did not work and, to add to her woes, her leg also had some sort of infection which had caused it to swell and there was an open sore behind her knee which clearly had been there for some time.

Kim had first met her the day before when she had approached the team teaching the ladies of the church. She had been prayed for but with no obvious improvement. Mombasa had come forward again, and when Kim had asked, "You're not healed, are you?" this young girl had shaken her head and requested, "Please fetch the man of God to pray." She had a very obvious expectation that God would move in her life.

As I laid hands on her, I felt God tell me to bend her knee, which I did. Her response was to scream out in pain and start to cry. I naturally felt terrible at causing her so much discomfort and could see many people in the church building had real concerns about what I had just done.

Nothing appeared to be any different; she still had no movement in the knee and I felt God say to me, "You need to bend it again." To say that I was not too confident in this course of action, mainly from fear of what the guys around me might do if I once again inflicted pain on this young girl, is an understatement! So, rather than bend the joint myself, I asked Mombasa to attempt some squats. This she did, very gingerly at first and then more quickly, declaring that she could now bend her knee.

We then went for a walk up and down the church hall after which I suggested that we might go for a run up the street. The street consisted of a mud road which was no more than six feet in width with an open sewer flanking either side. As it had been raining, the sewer had overflowed onto the street making it rather treacherous underfoot. We ran from the church building to the very end of the street and then started to return, still running at top speed. The slum was in near complete darkness and Mombasa and I managed to trip over a water pipe crossing the street. We fell headlong into the mud and my heart sank as I imagined what damage she might have done to herself, but as she raised her head from the mud, a big smile came to her face and she said, "I ran, I ran!" When we got up from the dirt track, the only thing that was hurt was my pride and Mombasa Dora was completely healed.

This young girl's name changed that evening; she was no longer "Mombasa Dora, the cripple girl" but rather she was now "Mombasa Dora, the girl who used to be crippled". I learned again that afternoon that sometimes you have to work a miracle![73] You don't need to invest in much of an advertising campaign for your healing crusade when you have a well-known young girl running through the slum telling everyone she meets why she can now walk and run and jump as freely as any child should.

The following night she was on the makeshift stage at the open-air meeting and everyone could see how God had healed her. The stage had been erected from an assortment of old timber. The structure was approximately five feet high and moved backwards and forwards and from side to side as you walked across it. This in itself was considerably disconcerting as you felt that at any moment it might collapse, throwing you into the congregation or impaling you on a broken timber. My concerns for my own wellbeing, though, paled into insignificance when I realised that the prayer team for the mission, a group of some eight ladies, had ensconced themselves under the stage. Every night they prayed under the makeshift structure for the whole of the meeting no matter what was taking place above their heads. This ranged from large choirs leading the congregation in worship, and dancers jumping and running from side to side, to me preaching and praying for the sick. These faithful women were under there covering everything in prayer and exercising more than a little faith that the stage would not collapse.

Each night people from the local churches supported the mission with drama, mime and other forms of creative presentations. One evening this caused more than a little disturbance amongst the English team members as we were standing at the side of the stage waiting for our time to minister. Suddenly stood at our side was a man with what appeared to be explosives attached to his body and a balaclava covering his face. It was clear that he was trying to make his way to the stage. Shock and horror appeared on the faces of those around us and started to spread to some members of the congregation. Penny, one of the more mature members of our team, laid eyes on this chap, screamed out loud and then set off down the path away from the stage at a pace someone fifty years younger would have been proud to have achieved. It was only at this point that the pastor appeared and reassured us that the 'suicide bomber'

---

[73] 1 Corinthians 12:28

was in fact part of the drama that was going to take place in just a few seconds. Penny's heart took quite some time to return to a normal rate!

Later that same evening, God spoke to me about a man who had damaged his back and was now unable to work. I spoke out this word of knowledge and asked if the man would come forward for prayer but he did not respond. Rather, five ladies, all having damaged their backs and unable to work, came forward. Yet I felt sure that God had spoken to me specifically about a man and so I asked again, "Is there a man here who has damaged his back and is now unable to work?"

I was perplexed as five more ladies responded and joined the women already standing by the stage. Still feeling sure that God had spoken to me about a male, I asked for a third time, "Is there a man here who has damaged his back and is now unable to work?"

At that precise moment a man in Muslim dress was walking past the meeting ground and heard my announcement, responded and came forward saying that I had just described his predicament.

As I came down off the stage to pray for him, God said to me, "I've already healed him." I told the man what Father had just said and asked him to try to move in ways that he could not before. The man started to dance all around in front of the stage and it was very clear that he was healed, much to his delight.

There were still ten ladies standing looking at me expectantly as if to say, "Doesn't God want to heal us as well?" Immediately the passage from Matthew 15:27 where the woman said to Jesus, "Even the dogs eat the crumbs that fall from [the] table," came to mind. This, I felt, was God confirming that He did indeed want to heal these ladies as well. I instructed them to test themselves in the same way that the gentleman had tested his body and nine were instantly healed. The tenth woman was healed as soon as we laid hands on her.

I learnt the following day that the man whose back was healed had returned home that evening to his father's house where he, his wife and children were living since he had lost his job due to his back injury. When he explained to his father that he had been healed at the crusade meeting and that he had given his life to Jesus, his father responded by throwing him and his young family out onto the streets. The angry father informed him that he would not have a Christian living under his roof. The next morning the pastor told us of what had happened. Unbeknown to him, I had been given a gift at church the Sunday before we left England. The person who gave it to me related how God had told them I would meet a family with an unexpected pressing need and that I was to give them this gift to meet that need. As the pastor explained what had happened and detailed what this family would need to pay in a deposit and rent for a house, I realised that the donated amount would meet this need almost exactly. I happily passed on the gift and committed myself to praying that the man would quickly find employment to enable him to continue to pay the rent on his new home. His healing, and God providing the money for a house, was a powerful testimony to his wife and she soon joined him in putting her faith in Jesus. Some while after we returned to England I received an email to tell me that the man had secured a job working in the Sudan, a nation where it is very difficult for Christians to go. Yet because of his Muslim background it was no problem for him. He had been sharing his newfound faith with the people he was working with, a mostly Muslim group. This had resulted in a number of them becoming Christians themselves and he was now leading a small church in his bedsit. God will find a way where it seems there is no way. Praise God!

God moved powerfully through the team as they ministered each day and when we returned to the UK we had all learned that sometimes you just have to 'play the hunch', as our senior pastor Derek had preached on, and see where God leads you. It is so important that we listen to His voice wherever we find ourselves and in whatever we are doing.

Chapter Twenty-Two

Fun and Faith

ON ANOTHER TRIP TO UGANDA we were delayed sixteen hours at Heathrow Airport as our plane had been cancelled due to a mechanical fault. We were eventually given tickets with a different carrier and arrived at Entebbe extremely tired by our extended travel time. On the journey from the airport to Kampala I realised that there was a campaign meeting planned that evening and that we were being taken directly to the event as they were still expecting me to minister. When we arrived the meeting was well under way and a few minutes later I found myself being ushered onto the stage to speak.

I cannot say that it was one of my finest moments as I struggled to get my thoughts together to preach the Gospel through an overwhelming blanket of weariness. It seemed that things were particularly difficult that evening and it felt as though the message was coming up against a brick wall. I knew in my spirit that we needed a supernatural breakthrough but also realised that of myself I had little to give. As I knew that our Father had declared to Moses that He was the "I am", He was reminding me that He was whatever I needed Him to be that moment. So through my tiredness I pushed in until I heard the Holy Spirit telling me to invite the lady with breast cancer to come forward so that God could heal her.

There were hundreds of people in front of me and I had not a clue in the natural if there was anyone there with breast cancer or whether it was just my imagination speaking to me. Seeking to be obedient, I invited anyone with breast cancer to come forward. One lady appeared at the side of the stage and was soon ushered up onto it. She told us that she had travelled all the way from Kenya that day for an appointment at the hospital in Kampala scheduled for the very next morning. She was staying with a friend in the city who had told her about the campaign and suggested that they come down to keep her mind off the impending appointment. She then told us that she had a huge lump in her breast and had been informed that she needed surgery. In front of the campaign crowd she lifted her blouse and revealed the breast with the growth. It seemed to have broken through the skin and was clearly visible. It looked awful and I had never seen anything like it before. I encouraged her to cover it again in an effort to protect her modesty; then we laid hands on her head and came against the work of the enemy in her body and proclaimed health and healing to her in Jesus' name. Nothing appeared to happen so I encouraged the lady that God had not brought her from Kenya and me from England to meet in Kampala to leave her sick.

The following evening at the beginning of the meeting she came forward again but this time her countenance had lifted and she was full of joy. Once again she lifted her blouse and revealed the breast. There was no sign of the huge growth that just twenty-four hours before had been disfiguring her. Indeed, on closer inspection there was no sign that it had ever been there. She then told us that when she went to bed the night before nothing appeared to have happened but that morning when she woke her bedding was covered with black goo. She realised that something had happened and thought that perhaps the lump had broken open. She was fearful to look to see what sort of mess her breast might be in now. Eventually she plucked up the courage to look in the mirror and was amazed to see no sign of the lump and only clean, fresh skin where the night before she had been so disfigured by the horrible growth. At her appointment that morning the doctors refused to believe that she had ever had a growth and gave her a clean bill of health. Needless to say any wall of resistance to the Gospel during the rest of the campaign was broken down and the floodgates were opened for many to be healed, delivered and saved. Praise God that when we come to the end of our resources we are only just at the beginning of our wonderful heavenly Father's abilities. He can do far more than we can imagine.

Uganda proved to be the door which God used to open other African nations to us. We have since travelled to Kenya, South Africa, Tanzania and Zanzibar.

Ministering from a place of weakness in Africa often seems to be the way of things. People are so keen to squeeze as much out of you as possible that the ministry programmes are packed full. I was asked to join a team from New Life in Harrogate going to Tanzania. On the night of our arrival we were asked to minister at a large church where the pastor announced to the people that it was going to be a "Holy Spirit anointing evening". The large auditorium was packed full with expectant people. Unfortunately, we had prepared to speak on a different subject! The team were all tired and as Tim, the team leader, was suffering from a splitting headache, it fell to me to minister. Unprepared as I was to speak that evening, I stepped to the front of the meeting and trusted God that He would supply all that I needed. Scripture after scripture about the Holy Spirit was brought to my remembrance and I spoke for over an hour. By the time I finished there was a tangible sense of the presence of the Holy Spirit in the auditorium. The team joined me as we started to pray for people to be filled with the Holy Spirit and, boy, were they! People were speaking in tongues, shaking, falling over and even laughing under the influence of the Spirit. Once again God proved to me that He only needs willing vessels. Kathryn Kuhlman once said, "God is not looking for clay vessels, He's not even looking for golden vessels; all He is looking for is willing vessels." He is looking for vessels to work through so that He might do wonderful things.

This trip also reminded me again that God wants us to enjoy ourselves! I have always been an adventurous sort of person and enjoy a challenge. Several years ago Kim bought me a four-wheel driving day run by Land Rover. It was great to get out into a field and put a Land Rover Defender through its paces, which culminated in driving over what appeared to be a cliff face and on down an incredibly steep incline. So when we were invited to drive out to a Masai tribe to preach I volunteered to drive one of the four-wheel vehicles. We drove along mud tracks, through rivers and over scrubland to reach our destination. Great fun! The tribe entertained us with a traditional Masai dance and we had a fantastic time with them and enjoyed a meal with the warriors after the service. By the time we left that evening it was dark, which upped the challenge of the return journey a notch or two. Trying to follow the lights of a four-wheel drive in front down muddy tracks, across scrubland and through rivers that wash over the bonnet when there is no ambient light is truly adventurous and not a little daunting. Praise God, we made it back to the hotel without any mishaps.

I have always harboured a dream of flying a plane. Before the time when plane cockpits were securely locked to prevent terrorist intrusion I would often ask if I could go up to the flight deck during a long haul flight and spend some time with the crew. When we boarded the little twelve-seater, twin engine, turboprop plane to fly down to Zanzibar I noticed that the co-pilot seat was empty. I asked the pilot if I might join him. He welcomed me and even encouraged me to put on the headphone and microphone set so we could talk. Just after take-off he asked me if I would like to fly the plane. Foolishly I replied, "I would love to!" never of course imagining that he would let me. To my amazement, the pilot flicked a switch and informed me that he had passed over control of the plane to me, and he took his hands off the controls. He then proceeded to give me a flying lesson. I continued to bring the plane to its cruising altitude then levelled it off; we then flew straight ahead for a while after which we banked to the right and I could see the Zanzibar Island below. The captain instructed me to drop our height and line the plane up with the runway which I very nervously did. On the final approach he flicked the switch to return the controls to himself and landed the plane. I am not sure whether the other eleven passengers realised what was going on but as no-one complained, I can only assume that they were all oblivious of just who was piloting them. Kim and I have a saying we often use to describe things like this: "Only in Africa..."

A number of ministries from Kenya had attended the conferences in Kampala and the following year we received an invitation to not only return to Uganda but also to travel on into Kenya to spend some time teaching in a church close to the Tanzanian border.

When telling people about missions I often half joke that they can be challenging times and people should expect God to work in them as well as through them. I believe we learn the most when we set our feet to get out of the church building and into the mission field, wherever that may be.

Our first trip to Kenya was no exception; challenges abounded! We entered the country shortly after elections had taken place and violence had erupted at perceived rigging of the vote. The situation was very tense and we were trying to keep a low profile.

We chose to stay in a hotel that was a little out of the town where we were ministering as the planned accommodation was within view of the border and the area left much to be desired as regards safety. For the first few days all went well apart from the normal discomforts of Africa: bad roads; no hot water or electricity; and very poor sanitation. The church that we were working with consisted of a compound with a large awning set up over benches for the people to hear us teach. Despite the church being very poor, daily they sought to feed those worse off than them. One evening, having spent the day ministering, we returned to our hotel, Sugarlands[74], and instead of going directly to the dining hall I noticed that the electricity was on, which meant the possibility of a hot shower. I encouraged the team to go to their rooms and take advantage of this as none of us had managed a hot shower in days!

This very quickly showed itself to be God's leading as we had not been in our rooms for more than a few minutes when the sound of automatic gun fire sounded out a number of times from the reception area below accompanied by much shouting. Kim and I retreated into the bathroom as it was the only part of our room that had solid walls. The team wisely stayed in their rooms and we all waited to see what would happen. After some minutes had passed with no further sound of gun fire, I phoned reception from my mobile phone to try to find out what was happening. I was assured that there was no problem and it was perfectly safe for us to come downstairs!

One by one, the team emerged and we met in the dining hall. The reception staff continued to assure us that there had been no problem, the noise was simply a car backfiring and everything was alright. So convincing were they in their denial that I began to wonder if we had all fallen prey to a bout of overactive imagination; until the waiter

---

[74] The hotel derives its name from the primary crop of the area surrounding the town: cane sugar.

came to take our order and he was obviously clearly agitated and happily spilled the whole story under gentle questioning.

Bandits had heard that a group of white people were staying at the hotel and had come in to try and rob us. They had shot up the reception area and had demanded to know where we were and our room numbers. Our little waiter had scared them off by walking into reception and telling them that he had called the police and they had better go before the officers arrived. He was the hero of the day, albeit very shaken up. We thanked God for our hot showers and the fact that we had been in our rooms instead of the dining hall as we would have normally been at that time of day. We were grateful for our quick-witted waiter – and he did well with his tips that evening! We will never know whether the police were in fact called out as they simply didn't put in an appearance.

Our waiter was quite a character. Every evening he would present us with menus full of tempting options. We soon realised that it saved a lot of time to simply ignore the menu and ask what the chef was cooking that evening. Invariably it was a chicken dish that did not even appear in said menu which was a work of fiction!

I often try to give the teams a day off during a mission and having spoken with our taxi driver, he assured me that the Masai Mara game park was only a two-hour journey from where we were staying. The team decided that they would very much like to visit the nature reserve and so we booked the minibus to come very early the next day so that we would be in the game park just after daybreak. We had been informed that this is the best time of day to see game.

Everything seemed to be going well and after travelling for an hour-and-a-half we saw a sign to the park and turned off the main road onto a smaller one in our little ten-seater minibus. We were all anticipating arriving at the park within half an hour or so. The road we were on got progressively narrower until eventually it petered out to a mud track and then changed again to what appeared to be a dried out riverbed, and then it disappeared altogether. Nearly two hours had passed since we had left the main road and there was still no sign of the park. We were now bumping along on open scrubland with no road and no signs, and our driver was looking more than a little worried. We did, however, come across a handmade "Diversion" sign which directed us around a large hole in the scrubland. Considering there was no visible road of any sort, this was both highly amusing and worrying at the same time!

Soon the dry scrub gave way to very wet scrub and the inevitable happened as the back wheels of our minibus sank up to their axles. Try as hard as we could, they were not coming out. The atmosphere in the minibus was deteriorating; we were in the middle of nowhere having not seen any other living soul in over two hours.

We were three-and-a-half hours into what was meant to be a two-hour drive when a group of Masai tribesmen came into view herding their cattle across the scrub. They were soon enlisted to help get the minibus out of the mud, and after grateful thanks and a quick enquiry as to where the road might be, we were directed to continue heading in the same direction until we saw a water tower in the distance and to then head for the structure. There we would find the road once more.

After an hour of bumping across the scrubland we finally spotted the water tower and forty minutes or so later we thankfully turned back onto a very rough dirt track and resumed our journey for the game park. On our approach we were met by a game warden who flagged us down and asked where we had come from. On furnishing him with the information he told us that we were lucky to have made it as he would not even consider taking his four-wheel drive Land Cruiser on that route!

However, he pointed us to the entrance of the game park nearby and so after nearly six hours' travel we finally arrived at our destination only to be told by the reception staff that we were very unlikely to see anything at this time of day – but we were welcome to hire a guide and go in as they were happy to relieve us of our US dollars! Having come this far, not one of us wanted to return without going in.

We transferred into the guide's four-wheel drive and entered the park. God is so good; within minutes of being there, much to the complete surprise of our guide, we spotted a herd of elephants and then a lone white rhino, which caused him much excitement. This vista of wildlife unfolded before us for the next two hours and we exited the park having seen all of the big five with the exception of the leopard and almost every other African animal you could imagine. Our guide was amazed and told us that guests who had been visiting for a week had often not seen all that we had experienced in the short time that we had been there. Our God is just so wonderful and we were all convinced that He had told the animals that His sons and daughters were passing through and they had lined up to see us!

Thankfully, our driver Ishmael had taken some directions from the park rangers and our return journey kept to the tarmac roads – but still took over five hours. We had boldly gone where no one should have ventured in a vehicle completely unsuited for the terrain but God had kept us safe, provided help when we needed it and given us the adventure of a lifetime. We were privileged to see many of the wonders of His creation and I think all of us once more at the end of the day realized that God really cares about His children and delights in giving good gifts.[75]

Taking days off in Africa should come with a government health warning! On a later mission in Kenya we were traveling near to a safari park with a day free in our schedule, which seemed just too good an opportunity to miss. A one-night stopover was planned so that the team could go into the park and enjoy the wildlife and countryside of this beautiful nation.

Unlike other parks we had visited on previous trips, this one encouraged you to take your own car in so we duly checked in with our nine-seater minibus. Driving along the well-worn tracks around the park revealed amazing scenery and we immediately began to catch sight of many of the wonderful animals that are native to Kenya. By lunchtime we had seen very many species of wildlife, including all of the big five with the exception of the lion. We considered ourselves very blessed as we sat to eat our lunch in one of the restaurants in the park. Keen to make sure the team went home having seen all the big five, I had noticed there were a couple of Masai Park rangers also having their lunch. I approached them to find out if they had any insider knowledge on where in the park we might have a good opportunity to see the lions and complete our tour. After a little discussion they pointed us to some hills on the far side of the park. Buoyed up with this information, we set off towards the hills which were around an hour's drive from the main entrance. As we climbed the hills in our minibus, the roads got wet and muddy

---

[75] See Matthew 7:11

until we eventually became completely bogged down in the mire, unable to move forward or reverse. We realised we had arrived in lion country. This left us with a bit of a dilemma as none of us wanted to leave the safety of the minibus to try and push it out of the mud, for concern over our safety.

After an hour it was clear that no one was going to answer our mobile phone calls to the ranger station for help and as it was starting to get dark, the thought of spending the night in a minibus in the middle of a safari park was not a very appealing one! Looking down the track I noticed two other minibuses also stuck in the mud and decided it was time to take action. I got out with a number of the guys on our team and we walked down to the other buses and agreed with them that if we all got out we could help each other to get our vehicles unstuck and leave the park before nightfall. While the ladies kept watch for lions, a group of about fifteen men from the three buses pushed the first two out of the mud but then, to our horror, the men from these buses announced that they needed to go now and could not help us get ours out of the mud! They got back in their buses and drove off promising to send help.

With the light fading fast and still no help appearing we had no choice but to try to move the bus on our own. So five men took on the task that needed fifteen. The mud was a foot deep and very sticky and we kept losing our shoes in it. So there we were, bare foot in deep mud, trying to be as quiet as possible while keeping one eye out for lions as we pushed and bounced our minibus, trying to find some traction, all the time praying for the Lord's strength.

Suddenly the bus gained the necessary traction and lurched forward, leaving some of us now lying prostrate in the mud. A unanimous cry went up of "Praise the Lord!" and we all ran to get on the vehicle, which we did not want to stop again out of concern of getting stuck once more. We made it to the main gate just after nightfall and a little before the park closed, for which we were all grateful. When we inquired why no one had come to help we were told that no one had reported that we had been stuck! Returning to our hotel that night we must have been a strange sight. We all learned something about trusting God that day and that with God nothing is impossible. Ours was the strength of Samson!

Traveling in Africa is always interesting and often challenging. On one trip from Uganda to Kenya we made the mistake of taking a Trans Africa coach. We were not expecting it to be anything like a National Express from back in the UK but, then again, I don't think any of us were expecting it to be quite as bad as it turned out to be. The coach looked as if it had been rescued from a war zone judging by the amount of external damage. The interior was not much better; seats were badly worn with foam rubber poking from the holes. Oblivious to health and safety considerations, additional fold down seats had been fitted in the gangway. Added to this were boxes and luggage which could not fit in the lockers or on the shelves above the seats. It would be impossible to exit the coach in a hurry in the event of an emergency. Under my seat I discovered a small cage housing three live chickens. Every seat was taken and as the bus made its way onto the main highway we soon became painfully aware that the suspension had seen better days and that the shock absorbers had probably gone altogether. It was set to be a very long eight hours. Our hopes of seeing the African countryside were also dashed as the thick cloud of dust that the coach whipped up meant it was virtually impossible to see anything out of the windows.

Our driver, however, was determined to keep us on schedule as he raced down the road beeping his horn and overtaking anything that he deemed to be going too slowly. On several occasions this meant that he overtook vehicles that were at the same time overtaking other vehicles. He achieved this by leaving the road and taking to the dirt verge on the wrong side of the road, much to the dismay of oncoming vehicles who on several occasions had to pass between us and the vehicles we were overtaking. All these manoeuvres were carried out with his foot to the floor. 'Terrifying' is an understatement to describe the emotion his antics roused in our English hearts! Yet all around me were Africans who had either lost consciousness from fear or who had simply fallen asleep and who, I assumed, had decided that it was better not to see what was happening.

The coach was also beginning to resemble the inside of an oven – the heat and smells were overwhelming – and soon all of us were overtaken by sleep just like our travel companions. We seemed to be making good time thanks to our crazy driver but eventually even he could not get past the biggest traffic jam I have ever seen in my life.

There were cars, buses and trucks as far as the eye could see stretched out on the road ahead of us. The road itself was only two lanes wide but the traffic jam ahead of us was at least three lanes wide in both directions as vehicles were swapping lanes trying to make headway.

Our planned eight-hour journey across Africa was supposed to conclude by us having a shower, a meal and a good night's sleep in a hotel in Kampala before we were to catch our plane back to the UK. This plan was in tatters. The journey morphed into a twenty-hour nightmare. Our constant confession was, "We are going to catch our plane," so it was no surprise, when we eventually arrived in Kampala, that we had enough time to grab a taxi minibus and get to the airport just before our gate was to close. Praise God, He kept us safe and got us there in time to get home. Trans Africa bus? Never again!

CHAPTER TWENTY-THREE

No Limits, No Boundaries

MEANWHILE, BACK AT HOME, in addition to setting up the Healing Hour in our church we were now receiving invitations to help other churches set up healing ministries and spent a lot of time training, equipping and encouraging them to go for more in God while sharing from the things we had learned.

This has been a great blessing – seeing believers around the world starting to experience for themselves the power of the Holy Spirit to heal and set people free from whatever the devil has bound them with. To hear the reports from these groups of the great things that God was doing among them as well as from our own teams was just wonderful. Our God is truly powerful and wants His children to be a people who are anointed with power from on high, not just in church on a Sunday morning but wherever we are, whatever we are doing. Whether you are at home or work, out with friends or just doing the shopping, we need to attune our lives to the Holy Spirit's leading.

One morning my friend John and I were coming out of a McDonald's that was sited in a basement in Bath. We were attending a conference in this spa town. As we were climbing the stairs, I noticed an older man bent over carrying his shopping on the stairs ahead of us. The gentleman was having to stop every few steps as he was clearly in some pain, making his ascent difficult. At this point the passage of scripture went through my head that "[Jesus] went about doing good"[76] so I suggested to John that we help this man. John offered to carry his shopping and I offered an arm to help him up the stairs. When we reached the top he thanked us and was about to carry on his way when, again, a voice in my head said, "Well, you got it half right!"

Shocked by this, I replied to God, "What do You mean?"

Father encouraged me to remember the whole of the scripture that had motivated us to help this man in the first place. It does, of course, say, "[Jesus] went about doing good..." but it continues, "...and healing all who were oppressed by the devil..."

I felt the Holy Spirit encouraging us to go a bit further with this guy. So I asked if he would mind if we prayed for him, an offer he accepted and then immediately started to walk away. It was clear that he had failed to realize that we wanted to pray for him there and then. I called him back and explained further what I had meant by the offer.

His response was to ask, "What, here, outside McDonald's?"

"Yes!" I replied and he rather reluctantly agreed.

Both John and I laid our hands on his shoulders and started to pray that God would heal his pain and straighten his spine. As we did this we began to draw a small crowd of people who were obviously wondering what we were doing. I became aware that some of them were probably concerned for this older gentleman as he appeared to be bent over under the hands of two burly chaps. It became clear to me that they thought that we might be mugging him and so I closed my eyes! As we prayed I felt my hand rise up and when we had finished praying I opened my eyes to see the man looking me full in the face. On enquiring how he was feeling, he replied, "Much better, thank you."

I encouraged him to attempt something that he could not previously do to which he replied, "I am!" I asked him what he meant and he explained that for the last few years he had not been able to stand up straight yet here he was now standing tall, no longer bent over and looking us in the eye. We blessed him and the three of us went on our separate ways rejoicing over what God had done for him there on the street outside McDonald's.

---

[76] Acts 10:38 (NASB)

A few days later, I was meeting a colleague Steve in a local café in Aldershot to discuss our upcoming ministry trip to the Balkans, over a coffee in a relaxed atmosphere. We had been chatting for an hour or so when he needed to go to the restroom.

While I was awaiting his return, I noticed a lady who was sitting at the next table looking at me with a quizzical expression on her face. So I greeted her and asked if she was enjoying the coffee. She assured me that she was and then asked if I would mind telling her what my colleague and I did for a living as she could not help but overhear our conversation. When I informed her that we were both church ministers she was somewhat surprised.

"You don't look much like ministers!" was her comment, which I took as a compliment. Within moments she opened up and told me her life history. It transpired that she was suffering with regular nightmares, amongst other things, which had upset her sleeping patterns and left her feeling very distressed. I offered to pray with her when my colleague returned from the restroom to which she readily agreed and there in the café we laid hands on her and bound whatever force was disturbing her sleep. After some further conversation about faith and Jesus she left.

Some months later I was in the same café with my wife and this lady came in the door. Seeing us there, she walked up to our table and exclaimed, "It's you, isn't it?" I did not recognise her until she reminded me of how my colleague and I had prayed with her and how since then she had not had any more nightmares and was feeling much more peaceful. Also the arthritis that had caused her much pain over the years was significantly improved. God had set her free that day and she knew it. After she left, Kim and I rejoiced at how great our God is.

I am learning that He wants to work much more than we can begin to imagine; we just need to keep our spirits attuned to hear Him speaking. I will often tell people that there are voices and pictures and even films flowing through the room constantly wherever we find ourselves; we can't see or hear them because we are unable to tune into them. If, however, we availed ourselves of a radio or a television set we would be able to receive them. I believe that is also true of God. He is talking much more than we imagine. He has given us a God 'receiver', the Holy Spirit, so that we can hear Him but because we so often walk around with our spirits out of tune with His Spirit, we often miss out on so much that He wants to do in us and through us. God once said to me, "Tim, I don't speak that quietly; it's just that you listen from so far away." Scripture tells us that if we will "draw near to God ... He will draw near to [us]"[77].

Jesus sent the Holy Spirit that we might know the mind of God and be the people He intended us to be in every situation. He doesn't just want to work in our meetings or our buildings blessing the Christians, He wants to work wherever we are, whatever we are doing. You only have to look at the life and ministry of Jesus and the disciples to recognize that. He is sitting at a well looking for a drink when a woman comes along.[78] He engages her in conversation out of which He ends up preaching to all the men of the village. He is passing by a funeral and turns it into a celebration as He raises the widow's son back to life.[79] Jesus did all this because He was open to the Holy Spirit's leading and wanted to carry out the will of His Father.

Peter and John are on their way to the Temple to pray.[80] They see a lame beggar and raise him up and heal him and we are told that the man walked and leaped and praised God as they continued on their way to the Temple. These miraculous events were never meant to just happen in our meetings but rather be a part of our everyday life, instigated by a people who walk around attuned to the will of God through the leading of the Holy Spirit. The Bible is not just a history book; it sets out examples that we are meant to follow and gives us guidance to keep us on the right path.

For many years when I travelled to warmer climes I would half-jokingly declare that I enjoyed visiting such countries because it increased my opportunity to see shadow healings! England is known worldwide for our wet weather so I would tell my foreign friends, "You don't get very good shadows in England so I have come here because you do. I'm expecting to see my shadow start to heal the sick

---

[77] James 4:8 (NASB)
[78] See John 4
[79] See Luke 7:12
[80] See Acts 3:1

because it says in the Bible that when Peter's shadow fell on the infirm as he passed by, they recovered!"[81]

Many years went by without me being aware of my shadow falling on anyone and them subsequently experiencing healing. Yet on a cold, wet winter's day in a small gypsy church in Bulgaria, the building illuminated by a single forty-watt bulb, a man responded to a call for salvation that I had made. Shortly after coming forward I noticed that he had a broad smile on his face which, for some reason, seemed odd to me. I knew that God was doing something more than just bringing salvation to this guy and so I enquired of him, "What's going on with you?"

He told me how for some years he had been suffering from arthritis throughout his body yet the moment he stepped into my shadow he felt all the pain drain from his body. He lifted his hands in demonstration and said, "Look, I can bend all my fingers without any pain!" and started to open and close his hands to prove it. I might have jokingly limited God to working in sunny climates with strong shadows but I was privileged to have my heart's desire to see God work again as in New Testament times realized. Even though He saw my desire, He wanted to show me that He was able to work way beyond my expectations and there, in a dimly lit room in a cold gypsy village in the middle of winter, a man walked into my shadow and God healed him. That is a lesson we would all do well to learn. We serve a God who wants us to recognize that His power is limitless and He wants to break out of the pathetic limitations we put on Him working in us and through us. Let us make it our goal not to limit Him anymore. Let Him out of the box! At this time, we held a confession in our church which still rings true in my spirit today: "No Limits, No Boundaries" – the song by Israel Houghton. God cannot be confined or restricted; such limitations only exist in our minds.

---

[81] See Acts 5:15

Chapter Twenty-Four

Angels Come in All Shapes and Sizes

ON RETURNING FROM A MINISTRY TRIP to Uganda with a team from our home church, I was giving a short report to our church during the Sunday morning meeting, telling them how the church we were working with in Kampala was active among the people in the slums and caring for orphans by taking them into their homes. These people had next to nothing yet they were still showing God's love to the people around them. There was a spontaneous reaction from our people, wanting to help, so we set up a child sponsorship programme to help the church in Kampala meet the needs of orphans. Thirty to forty children were taken on that day and sponsored as we as a church sought to meet the needs of those less fortunate than ourselves. All of us who had been part of the team that had gone to Uganda were so humbled by our brothers' and sisters' response; it was such a blessing.

Little did we envisage the problems that such a sponsorship programme would cause! It almost tore the church in Kampala to pieces. Not many months into the launch of the programme, rumours began to circulate in the slum that more money was being sent than was reaching the people. The people believed that there are limitless resources in the church in the UK and didn't understand why not all of their children could be sponsored. All this caused much confusion and distrust with people believing different stories, and eventually emails started to filter back to England containing accusations of mismanagement of the funds.

It soon became apparent that someone needed to visit Kampala to resolve the situation. Kim and I agreed that we would cut short our holiday in South Africa and fly up to Uganda to talk with everyone involved. After several days of discussion and prayer with the people there, it became clear that we would never untangle all the accusations and counter-accusations.

I said to Kim that I simply did not know whom to believe, to which she pointed out that we were in need of the wisdom of Solomon. I recognised in that moment that this was a word from God and I now knew what we needed to do. The next morning, we all met again and I announced that due to the lack of unity, I had decided that it was better to close the child sponsorship programme and that I would be taking what remained of the money back to the UK to be returned to the sponsors. At this, the roomful of people divided into two groups: one agreeing loudly with me and telling me to take the money and leave the country; the other group started to beg me to change my mind and asked me to give control of the project to the opposing group but not to let the children have this opportunity taken from them. In a moment we knew who was telling the truth and just who had a heart for the children. I then explained that we would continue the project and would form a management group from the people who were putting the children first. I informed them that I would go into the slum the very next day to announce how the project was to progress. We closed the meeting and felt that God had shown us the way forward.

As we relaxed in our hotel room that evening we thanked God that we had seemed to have found a righteous solution. Little did we know what the morning would bring! We received notification from Reception telling us that there was a telephone call waiting for us but that the caller would not give his name. Did we wish to speak with him? Thinking that it was someone calling to rearrange our pick up time, which was not an uncommon occurrence, I took the call. The moment the call was transferred I realised that this was not the case! The man on the other end of the line immediately started shouting at me and threatened that if we went to the village that morning they would kill us, and then the line went dead before I could attempt any reply.

This was a very disturbing message, especially as we knew that when tempers were lost in Kampala people were very often murdered. We had experienced this on a previous trip. We had been in the town looking to buy a motorbike for Pastor Joel. We visited one shop and were moving to another because they did not stock the model he wanted. Our taxi driver drove us through a demonstration. As we made slow progress, people were leaning in the taxi windows declaring, rather menacingly, "You're not getting home tonight!" As we eventually left the crowd behind and turned the corner, we realized that the police were expecting a confrontation as a large group of riot police were stationed in the next road. We eventually bought the motorbike and returned to our hotel to great sighs of relief. We heard later that when the demonstrators had reached the first shop we had been to, frustrations boiled over and a number of employees were dragged from the shop and hacked to death on the street because they were foreign nationals. At this time there was a strong resentment towards outsiders. Everyone at the hotel had known that we were going to this shop and were worried that we had been caught up in the troubles there. Thank God that we had left the shop just minutes before the killings took place!

So, sitting in our hotel room some months later having received this call we were left wondering whether it was wise to go into the village. I decided to text our church leader Derek and ask what he thought we should do. Immediately we received his reply saying that the church, who were meeting at that very moment, had prayed and that, "God is sending a big angel to protect you."

My reply was, "That's all very well for you to say sitting in church back in the UK!" I told Kim that she did not need to come with me that morning but she would not hear of me going on my own. So we set out to the village. On our arrival we were met by the head man. He was wearing his hat signifying his status as chief elder and was carrying his staff of authority and assured us of our safety. He explained that he had heard about the threat on our lives. He was a Muslim man but because our project was helping orphans from any and every background he was very pleased with it and so had arrived to offer his protection. Angels come in all shapes and sizes! Our angel was our shadow as we went about our business in the village. Everything went well that morning and a measure of peace returned to the project that day.

The need in this part of Africa is far greater than any of us can imagine and can be overwhelming as we realise that none of us can meet it on our own. I am reminded of the story of the thousands upon thousands of starfish that were washed up on the beach after a great storm. A young boy was walking along the beach picking them up and throwing them back into the sea one by one. An old man came along and shouted out to him that he was wasting his time, that he wasn't making any difference to the masses of starfish dying in the morning light. The boy simply bent down and picked up another starfish and threw it back into the sea and called back, "I made a difference to that one!" and then he threw another back into the water and shouted out, "And I made a difference to that one!" and so he continued along the beach, set on his task of making as big a difference as he could.

If we can only see the big picture, we will often fail to see what we as individuals can do. Each of us has a role to play and if we all do our part we can affect the bigger picture. Our part might seem insignificant but together we can make a change. We have to trust God and do our part and He will do His as He did that morning in Kampala by sending an angel to protect us. He will bring all the parts together to make a difference.

CHAPTER TWENTY-FIVE

Commanded to Hear the Gospel

BACK IN THE UK I WAS FEELING that God wanted to stretch us again. I felt Him leading me to look into buying a bigger tent. I was not at all sure about this so decided I would wait until I was thoroughly convinced that I had heard Him clearly!

One Sunday morning while preaching I related how I found myself in this quandary to illustrate a point I was making. To my horror, two people walked up to me afterwards and said that they had felt for a while that I should buy a bigger tent and both offered to donate funds towards its cost. I quickly explained that, no, at this time I was not at all sure whether I would pursue this project and that they should keep their money. If and when I did get clear leading from the Lord then, at some later stage, I would come back to them.

Their parting comment of, "The money will be waiting for you when you are ready," was both a blessing and a pressure! A blessing that they wished to sow into a new venture in God and a pressure in me having to determine exactly what Father was saying about it all.

Over the next few months I did not talk to God about the subject as, frankly, I did not want to hear what He might have to say about it all. One morning, however, I awoke to hear God's voice telling me that I needed to buy a bigger tent, that it was already in the UK, was not currently being used and that I should make an offer on it.

I pondered on just how you would find a second-hand large tent in the UK. I decided to phone Miami Missionary Tents in the States where we had previously purchased our two tents. I enquired whether the company had supplied any tents bigger than ours to the UK, expecting them to give me a list. However, their reply made things easy as they had only supplied one bigger than ours and were happy to furnish me with the phone number of the church that had bought it.

The next morning, I phoned the church in Brentwood and said that I understood that they had a big tent for sale. The line went quiet and then the voice enquired, "How did you know?"

I explained what God had said to me and then the guy told me that they had just had a meeting the day before in which they had decided they should sell the tent. When I asked how much they wanted I was told, "Twenty-five thousand pounds." This figure was way beyond the fifteen hundred pounds I had been promised on that Sunday morning. I explained that I had nowhere near that sort of money but assured them I would come back if I ever did!

I breathed a sigh of relief. I did not pray for the requisite funds because although I now knew God wanted me to buy the tent, I was still not convinced that I was up for the challenge.

Within a couple of weeks Brentwood came back to me and told me that they were so sure that God wanted me to have the tent that they would drop the price to the fifteen thousand pounds that I had. At this point I explained that they must have misheard me as I only had fifteen *hundred* pounds. Their reply was gracious in shortness: "Well, we can't let you have it for that!"

Again, as I put the phone down I breathed a sigh of relief and still refused to talk to God about it or even think about this tent. In truth the idea frightened me and I wanted nothing to do with it. God, however, had other ideas. Within a couple of weeks, I had been given the fifteen thousand pounds needed to purchase the big top. I could feel God was pushing me towards buying it but I was still not convinced I wanted to go that way. So when I phoned to say that I now had the money to buy the tent I insisted that the Brentwood church put it up so I could inspect it before the deal went through.

To be honest, I was hoping that there would be some legitimate reason on inspecting the giant canvas which would justify my polite refusal to purchase. Because of my diary and their commitments, we could not arrange this viewing for a couple of months and I continued to hope that it would fall through.

Eventually the fateful day arrived and a group of us travelled to Essex to see the tent go up and learn how to erect the canvas. When the big top stood before me it was truly massive. If my colleagues had thought the previous tent was too big then what were they going to think of this one which was over twice the size?

Of course, as you have probably already guessed, there was nothing defective with the tent and so my loophole closed and that day we packed it up, loaded the equipment into our trucks and returned home with it.

Strangely, all those who came up with me that day seemed excited about it but I have to admit I was still very apprehensive and not at all sure about what God was so clearly leading me into.

Having purchased the new tent, we needed to kit it out so that we could start to use it. It seemed to me that all the work involved in putting up the tent just so we could wire it out for lighting and power was not a wise use of time. It seemed sensible to host an evangelistic event at the same time. Despite all the travelling I undertake, my desire has always been to bless the churches in my local area. The only site near to where I live that is large enough to erect a tent of the size of our big top is on ground owned by the Army. I asked my friend John Cook, who at that time was heading up Aldershot Churches Together (ACTs), if he had any contacts into the Army and he informed me that he knew the chaplain for the garrison and was happy to arrange a meeting.

A few days later we met with Tim Cole in his office and I explained my vision to put on a big evangelistic event in the area that would be a blessing to the whole community. To my surprise he was instantly enthusiastic, which I considered to be a miracle as we were from very different spectrums of the church. Within a week we were meeting with the garrison commander (who was not a Christian) and pitching our plans for a weekend evangelistic tent event that would reach out into both the civilian and Army communities. His permission to use the land was essential to the event going forward. Again I could see that God had already prepared the way for us. He explained that he was under orders to provide certain things for the soldiers' wellbeing – physically, mentally and spiritually – and if our event went ahead, for the first time in his posting he would feel comfortable ticking the 'spiritual' box. So permission was granted and it looked like everything was going to go ahead without any major hiccups.

It was about this time that our friend Keith shared a vision with me in which he saw Kim and me driving a small, old, battered car over a single carriageway bridge. He told me that it appeared as if the whole of the British Army was trying to come over the bridge from the opposite direction but that we refused to give way and were forcing them to reverse back so that we could cross the bridge. He told me that at the point at which we crossed the bridge the traffic flow on the bridge changed direction and was now all flowing in the direction in which we were travelling.

This vision meant little to me as things seemed to be progressing so well. Almost all the garrison chaplains were on-board with our vision and many of the local ministers had also committed their support. Along with the garrison commander's permission to use the land this all seemed to be the green light to go ahead, so we started to spend money from our own personal account as at this stage none of the churches had done more than commit to support the event with their time and people. We were happy to do this as we saw it as one of our steps of faith towards the event. The sums were not really that large, just a few thousand pounds, but all the same it was not the sort of money we had in our bank account.

It was at this time that the company that were responsible for the Army grounds stepped in. Initially they had informed us that we would need to pay twenty thousand pounds for the use of the land for the weekend and that we would also need to meet all their regulations in regard to the use of the land for an event of the size we were planning. We have always sought to meet local authority regulations regarding health and safety for events but this was clearly a whole new level. The commanding officer told us that their demands for twenty thousand pounds were out of the question and he would 'fix' that but we would indeed need to meet all the required regulations. With a little research we were able to provide the relevant documents required and the cost was reduced to six hundred pounds as standing orders for the garrison were to encourage community use of the Army land.

Unfortunately, the company who were responsible for the Army grounds had a contract saying that they must get the market value for use of any such grounds. This was in direct conflict with the garrison standing orders and so we became the ping-pong ball that was being knocked backwards and forwards between the Army and the company with the contract. On top of this, a call to the local authority after they had been in possession of our paperwork for nearly two months revealed that they had questions over what permissions we needed in order to put on the event and that they had decided we needed an Entertainment Licence, which they had failed to tell us about!

I was informed this would take thirty days to process and we now only had thirty-one days before our event was to go ahead. The forms for the licence were emailed to me along with a document explaining everything, which seemed to be about an inch thick. All this had to be read and inwardly digested, forms filled out, drawings of how we planned to set up the site to 100th scale drawn – all this in less than twenty-four hours and it had to be delivered to nine different agencies by the time their offices opened the next morning. It had to be right the first time as we had no time for a second application. It was just as well that it was my birthday and Kim and I had planned to spend the day together relaxing in the countryside to celebrate, otherwise we would have been booked up doing other things. We worked all day and most of the night reading the explanatory document, filling out the forms and drawing the scale drawings. As dawn broke I placed the completed paperwork into the envelopes and set off to deliver the nine packages to the various agencies around the county. We had given it our best shot and now all we could do was wait and pray. However, the company with the contract for the Army lands had one more shot to fire our way and they made an objection to our application for permission for the Entertainment Licence; this meant that two days before the event was to go ahead we were called into the council offices for a Safety Advisory Group meeting.

I sat on one side of a conference table with Tim the Army chaplain and the garrison commander's representative. On the other side were representatives from the nine agencies we had applied to and two guys from the company that looked after the Army contract and had to gain income from the Army land who had made the objection. It felt as if I was grilled forever but two hours later we left the room with the assurance that our licence would be granted and our event could go ahead.

What an event it was! In addition to all the friends who volunteered to help over the weekend, a group of soldiers were sent down to help put up the tent. The Army delivered two thousand chairs for us to use, saving us the rental costs. Breakfast was cooked and served by the Welsh guards for nine hundred soldiers on the Saturday morning, all of whom were commanded to be there to hear the Gospel preached by Mark who was ex British Special Services. He told how having achieved everything that most of the young men and women in the tent would only ever dream of doing, he had invited Jesus into his life as Lord and Saviour. You could have heard a pin drop as he declared this. We saw people healed and saved and around two thousand five hundred people came together to worship God on the Sunday morning, many of whom had never been to anything like it before.

At the end of the event the Garrison commander came over to me and said, "You will do this event again next year, won't you?" which was less of a question than an assertion. When I explained that I was not in his Army, he laughed and repeated the order. After speaking to my supreme commander I agreed with the commander that we would host the event the following year and again the year after that.

The chaplain Tim, whom I met that first day in his office and who was such a great help, wrote to me shortly after the event and told me how the event had changed his view of his role of being a chaplain. Up until the event he had considered it to be primarily a pastoral role but the event had impressed upon him that it could be an evangelistic one as well. It was a door that opened at a time when many of our young military personnel were being sent into frontline situations and were clearly thinking about the big questions of life. What a privilege it was to give them the opportunity to hear the Good News just before they were deployed. We can never be sure how many of them chose to follow the Lord over those weekends but I do know those chaplains who were involved are now not just pastors but evangelists as well. In a sense things did change forever for many who were involved and attended. For others, they failed to understand the ramifications of all that God did during these events. One local minister commented that we had taken his Sunday offering as he had not had a service but had come to the tent with his congregation. This saddened me, that he failed to see the bigger picture and gave so grudgingly. I hope his people didn't feel the same.

CHAPTER TWENTY-SIX

Our Source of Supply

THE NEW TENT ALSO GAVE US the opportunity to serve other people's visions. I was asked to take the tents to be the venue for the British Mighty Men's Conference with Angus Buchan in Yorkshire. It was great to meet with and help organise an event with a group of brothers who all had a desire to serve the body of Christ in our nation. We met together for six months and much of what I had learnt in putting on the events in Aldershot helped with the planning of this venture.

In its culmination a small group of my friends and the team of us who had organised the event stood in a field in Yorkshire – twenty of us in all, with two big tops to erect. It seemed that we were short on labour but at the end of two days both tents were up and ready for the nearly two thousand brothers from around the nation who came to be taught and inspired by Angus. What a privilege it was to be part of this event.

Over thirty men gave their lives to Jesus during the weekend and it was not even meant to be an evangelistic event, but I guess that's just the consequence of being together in one place in one accord; the Gospel is preached and the kingdom is expanded.

The planning for the event was much easier than for other events I have hosted in the big top. We had always wanted the event to be free to those who attended and had decided that we would only take up an offering on the Sunday morning. We determined that we would not count it until the event was finished and everyone had left the site. We had always trusted that God would supply what we had already spent to put the event on. No one on the team had the financial means to put on an event like this but we all felt the vision was right. It was a little surprising then, when we counted the offering, that we found that it was only twenty-five thousand pounds – not even half of what we had paid to put the event on. Undeterred, we agreed together that we had always trusted God to provide the money to cover the costs of the event and, without telling anyone from outside the planning group, we prayed and trusted God to meet our bills. Over the next six weeks every bill was paid on time. Praise God!

CHAPTER TWENTY-SEVEN

Will You Trust God?

OVER THE YEARS I HAVE BEEN involved in things I never imagined I would do. I've travelled the world preaching the Gospel and have seen thousands come to accept Jesus as their Lord and Saviour. Just as God said I would. There have been disappointments and some failures but I have come to realise that these are the battle scars of people who are seeking to move on with God.

Theodore Roosevelt said, "It is not the critic who counts; not the man who points out how the strong man stumbles, or where the doer of deeds could have done them better. The credit belongs to the man who is actually in the arena, whose face is marred by dust and sweat and blood; who strives valiantly; who errs, who comes short again and again, because there is no effort without error and shortcoming; but who does actually strive to do the deeds; who knows great enthusiasms, the great devotions; who spends himself in a worthy cause; who at the best knows in the end the triumph of high achievement, and who at the worst, if he fails, at least fails while daring greatly, so that his place shall never be with those cold and timid souls who neither know victory nor defeat."

I know that I have much left to do and I am seeking to press on to take hold of everything that Christ took hold of me to do.[82] I want to

---

[82] See Philippians 3:12

167

run in such a way as to win the prize.[83] I have also learnt that the Christian walk is not as complicated as some seem to think it is. The truth I declared to my youth group leader rather arrogantly all those years ago is still basically the key: "I have noticed that most Christians hear God but many fail to do what God tells them to do and so just slow their progress or don't move on at all." Arguments with God are pointless; He always wins. They only slow our progression into all that He has for us and result in us missing out on the some of the blessing He wants us to have.

Basically we need to do two things to live this Christian life.

Firstly, we need to hear what God is saying – He wants to speak with each and every one of us. He sent His Son into this world to make a way for each of us to enter into the Holy of Holies, the place where previously only a priest could enter. When Jesus died on the cross the veil in the Temple was torn from top to bottom, opening the way for us to go into God's presence and talk with Him. It was not torn from bottom to top for that might have been the work of a man; it was torn from top to bottom as only God could do that. He sent His one and only Son that we might enter into a relationship with Him, so you can be sure He wants to speak with you! Whoever you are, no matter what you have done or have not done, God wants to talk with you. I have discovered that He is talking far more than we can imagine. As I have already written, there are probably voices and films flowing past you right now but you cannot see or hear them because you need a receiver like a TV or radio switched on and tuned in to see and hear them. The same is true with God. We need to tune in to His channel to hear what He is saying. The Bible tells us that if we draw near to God, He *will* draw near to us.[84] He did not pay the ultimate price to have a relationship with you in order to stay quiet. He is talking; we need to tune in and hear what He is saying. Jesus said in Mark 4:8, "He who has ears to hear, let him hear."

Secondly, we need to do whatever He says. As we take each step of obedience there is no telling where it might take us. I have experienced this so often. What seem to be the most insignificant small steps open doors that you could never have imagined. I am reminded of the words of Neil Armstrong: "One small step for a

---

[83] See 1 Corinthians 9:24
[84] See James 4:8

man, one giant leap for mankind." Small steps in the kingdom can have unimaginable ramifications for our lives, just as failure to take those steps of faith can. Remember the guys who chose not to go back and fold their sheets? James 1:22 in the Message says, "Don't fool yourself into thinking that you are a listener when you are anything but, letting the Word go in one ear and out the other. Act on what you hear!" (MSG)

I want to encourage you that when you hear that voice, no matter how quiet or insignificant it seems, just do what He says. Only God knows what doors those steps of obedience will be the key to opening. Jesus said of the centurion that he had great faith because he recognized the significance of being under authority. Some have said that to me – that I am a man of great faith – but I know that I am just a man who is willing to do the things God has told me to do. So I have been privileged to see my God do some amazing things but not because I am anyone great. I am just an ordinary guy from a working class family who is seeking to hear what God is saying and, with as few arguments as possible, to just get on with what He says. There will always be people who seem to be doing more than you, just as there will always be those who appear to be doing less. Do not compare yourself with either as the only test we need to make is, are we hearing and doing the things God is telling us to do today? The past does not matter as we cannot change anything there as much as we might like to. The future is not worth worrying about. God has that all in control and one word from Him can change everything. If you are sick, it can heal you. If you are depressed or in bondage, it can set you free. Listen for His voice. He wants to talk with you. Do what He tells you and watch as He transforms your life and the lives of those you come into contact with. It will not always be easy and sometimes it will be plain hard, sometimes it will be scary, sometimes it will even be exhilarating and amazing, but all the time He will be with you. Just as He said to Joshua, "...I will be with you; I will never leave you nor forsake you."[85]

Some say that when the going gets tough, the tough get going. I prefer Daniel 11:32: "...but the people that know their God shall be strong, and do exploits." What has God got for you to do?

---

[85] Joshua 1:5

I often think about the story of the great French tightrope walker and showman Charles Blondin or 'The Great Blondini' as he was known. He once set up a tightrope over Niagara Falls. A huge crowd came to watch him walk over it. He played the crowd and asked if they thought he could do it to which they answered, "Of course you can!" He then walked over the Falls and back again, stopping halfway across to admire the view. Then he asked the crowd if they thought he could walk over and back pushing a wheelbarrow to which the crowd replied, "Of course you can! Of course you can!" He then upped the stakes by asking if they thought he could walk across and back pushing a wheelbarrow with someone in it. Again the crowd roared, "Of course you can! Of course you can!"

Finally, Charles asked the crowd, "Who will get in the wheelbarrow?" The crowd fell strangely quiet and no one answered. Then a little old lady pushed her way through the crowd and declared she would sit in the wheelbarrow. It was Charles' mother. Blondin pushed her over the Falls on the tightrope and back, much to the crowd's relief and amusement.

I think this story defines so much of what the Christian life is about. Will we respond to God's call to get in His wheelbarrow and put our trust solely in Him to take us wherever He has planned for us to go and do whatever He has planned for us to do?

Over the years we have learned many lessons and it seems that now we are using those lessons every time we step out onto a mission field as well as back home in the UK.

Let me encourage you to be of the same heart, just as Caleb and Joshua entered into everything that God promised them[86] because they were men of a different spirit and followed God wholeheartedly. We should continually listen for His voice, trust in His faithfulness and seek to carry out what He instructs us to do, being effectual doers of the word and not forgetful hearers.[87]

Wherever we find ourselves on our journey with God, let us be looking for new adventures of faith to see the further establishment of His kingdom in us and through us to the world we find ourselves in.

Let us always remember that we "are a chosen people, a royal priesthood, a holy nation, God's special possession, that [we] may

---

[86] See Numbers 14:24
[87] See James 1:25

declare the praises of him who called [us] out of darkness into his wonderful light"[88].

Remember, we are God's mighty men and women born for this hour!

---

[88] 1 Peter 2:9

Contact the Author

To contact the author, please send an email to:

admin@spearhead.org.uk

More information can be found online:

www.spearhead.org.uk

Or scan this with your smartphone to get to the website:

Recommended by the Publisher

Equipped to Heal
Ian Andrews
ISBN 978-1-907509-17-9

This is a day of great opportunities. In a time of uncertainty and despair, God is moving in power through his church across the world. Stories of conversions and healings are coming from the least likely places.

We can change the course of our world by first allowing change to overcome us so that we can become people-changers in turn.

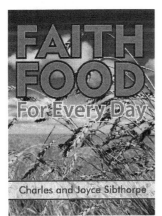

Faith Food for Every Day
Charles and Joyce Sibthorpe
ISBN 978-1-907509-63-6

A beautiful daily devotional, endorsed by a wide range of well-known Christian leaders. Each day you will find a message that will encourage your faith, help with the challenge of the day ahead, and stir you to develop your personal relationship with God.

Books available from
www.onwardsandupwards.org